Freedom from Religiosity and Judgmentalism:
Studies in Paul's Letter to the Galatians

Published by Kindred Productions, Winnipeg, Manitoba
1310 Taylor Avenue, R3M 3Z6, Canada

Printed in United States of America by Lightning Source

Cover design by Carson Samson. Plate image courtesy of Adobe Stock.
Page design by Galley Creative Co.

Library and Archives Canada Cataloguing in Publication
Title: Freedom from religiosity and judgmentalism :
studies in Paul's letter to the Galatians /
Mark D. Baker.
Names: Baker, Mark D. (Mark David), 1957- author.
Series: Luminaire studies.
Description: First edition. | Series statement: Luminaire studies |
Includes bibliographical references.
Identifiers: Canadiana 20230156312 | ISBN 9781894791588 (softcover)
Subjects: LCSH: Bible. Galatians—Commentaries.
Classification: LCC BS2685.3 .B35 2023 | DDC 227/.407—dc23

ISBN: 978-1-894791-58-8

Praise for *Freedom from Religiosity and Judgmentalism*

Baker's exploration of Galatians makes the ancient seem strikingly contemporary and the distant feel close to home. Recovering Paul's pastoral voice, Baker invites us to see how the grace of God revealed in Jesus radically transforms our ways of being together. Baker illuminates Paul's answer to the question of what it will take to see a fractured church gathered at one table

—*Meghan Good, Trinity Mennonite Church, Glendale, AZ*

Opening up Paul's letter by centering on the story of the Galatian churches to which it was written, this passionate commentary is an invitation to rediscover Paul's radical gospel of boundary-breaking grace. The fruit of decades studying and teaching Galatians in a variety of cultural contexts, Baker's book draws twenty-first century readers into Paul's first-century world to encounter anew his vision of Christ-centered community—a vision as challenging and life-giving now as it was then. Rich in theological insight and pastoral wisdom, this will be an excellent resource both for those who are reading Galatians for the first time and those who have been reading it all their lives.

—*Ryan Schellenberg, Ph.D., Author of*
Abject Joy: Paul, Prison, and the Art of Making Do

I was exploding with excitement in my soul as I read this book. It's an accessible, creative and indispensable commentary on Galatians. Baker helps us look through the lens of the center-set concept, highlighting how the church in Galatia and most churches today continue to fall into bounded & fuzzy-set traps. This welcomed and fresh approach to biblical scholarship brings the story of Galatians to our modern world, encouraging us to be authentic Jesus followers—creating space at the table for everyone. Baker has given me the inspiration to help those I lead say goodbye to judgmentalism and religiosity. There's nothing else like it—absolutely brilliant!

—*Jon Maurer, Foothill Vineyard Church, San Dimas, CA*

For more than two decades, Mark Baker has been writing books and teaching courses on Galatians to audiences in universities and seminaries, neighborhoods and prisons, churches and home Bible studies across North and South America. I am delighted to see the work of this insightful interpreter and gifted teacher now made available to an even wider circle of readers. With crystal-clear exposition, vivid imagery and illuminating analogies, Baker brings Paul's gospel to life for contemporary audiences. He summons us to a transformative encounter with the God who in Jesus Christ liberates human beings from the shackles of boundary-drawing religiosity and by his Spirit frees them for genuine community centered on living together as God's beloved children.

—*Ross Wagner Ph.D., Duke Divinity School*

Written in a style that is commentary, Bible study, and small group discussion guide all in one, this resource is accessible to learners of all backgrounds. Baker's perspective on Galatians focuses on our unity in Christ and provides a way forward for Christians exhausted by the many lines currently dividing His church.

—*Heather Perkins, Journey Church, Wichita, KS*

This book will add layers to your understanding of the tension in Galata. Two competing views of grace. Two competing views of freedom. Two conflicting church cultures: bounded set religiosity vs centered set faith. Mark Baker knits together the Apostle Paul's passionate call to the Galatian church, and to us, to embody the unexpected grace and liberating freedom found uniquely in Jesus—and the primacy of a Jesus-centric culture. A highly readable book.

—*Dan Serdahl, Newlife Church on the Peninsula, WA*

With this book, Mark Baker carries Paul's message to the Galatians forward to a new generation. How do we live in the truth of the Gospel without eventually adding our own customs, cultural value systems, ethnicity, or nationality as the markers and protectors of the Christian identity? Baker guides us by lifting the veil of culture, traditions, religion, and meaning of words during the time of the Apostle Paul's writing to the Galatians. The reflection questions are valuable gems. This book is a must for anyone drawn to understand and live in the grace of Jesus.

—*Malia Mooradian, Christ-Centered Freedom Ministries*

Freedom from Religiosity and Judgmentalism

Studies in Paul's Letter to the Galatians

MARK D. BAKER

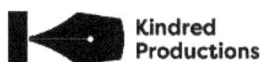

Kindred
Productions

WINNIPEG, MANITOBA

This book is dedicated to
my Pauline scholar friends:
Audrey, Ross, Jon, Ryan, Andy, Amy

Contents

Introduction

In my first fifteen or so years of ministry I valued Galatians, but I had no passion for it. I would turn to it when I sensed someone did not clearly understand that salvation is by God's grace, not human works. I thought it was an important book for someone like that, not so important for me.

That changed in 1992. I was preparing to lead studies on Galatians in a church in a squatter neighborhood in Tegucigalpa, Honduras. As part of my preparation I read an essay on Galatians by Richard Hays (Hays 1986). The essay invited me to reimagine the way I thought about the problem Paul addresses in Galatians—including some of the ideas I present in the first two chapters of this book. Through these new lenses I saw the letter in a way I never had before. I also sensed that God had important things to say to me through the letter. The Honduran church and I had a rich time studying Galatians together. It provoked dramatic changes in their church and a desire to understand more about this significant letter. Thankfully I had the opportunity to study

Galatians with Richard Hays while working on my PhD in theology. I shared my new insights with the church in Honduras and the growth and change continued.

Another key moment in my adventure with Galatians was reading Paul Hiebert's work on bounded, fuzzy, and centered churches (Hiebert 1978; 1994). Fittingly, I read this in 2000 while teaching at Mennonite Brethren Biblical Seminary (MBBS), now Fresno Pacific Biblical Seminary (FPBS), where Hiebert himself had studied. I began using Hiebert's work as a lens for interpreting Galatians. It has paid rich dividends and energized me even more to study and teach Galatians. I will introduce you to this lens in the first chapter of the book.

Since then I have led workshops on Galatians in various church settings, from Edmonton, Alberta to Huancayo, Peru, from Fresno, California, to Ethiopia. I have taught Galatians as a seminary course at MBBS/FPBS, in Tegucigalpa, Honduras and Bogota, Columbia. I have written a scholarly commentary on Galatians in Spanish (M. Baker 2014), preached sermons on Galatians, and lead Bible studies on Galatians in the Fresno County Jail. Yet even after all of that I continue to learn new things and God continues to speak to me through the letter. I am energized by the promise of learning and growing through writing this commentary and excited to share with you insights that have made this such an important book in my life and ministry.

May God's Spirit speak to you through Galatians; through this book may you experience in new and profound ways the liberating work of Jesus Christ, and through engaging the book with others may your church community become more centered on Jesus. May it become a community of radical unity and transformation through Jesus Christ.

Structure of this Commentary

Provoked by a problem of serious concern, Paul wrote a passionate letter to Galatian churches. His letter has wonderful potential to lead us to more deeply experience the liberating work of Jesus Christ individually and as church communities. The more fully we understand the situation that motivated Paul to write the letter, the more fully we will grasp and experience the freedom Paul proclaims. Therefore, the first two chapters of this book will lay a foundation for interpreting the letter by describing the problem, putting the letter in context, and providing key interpretative lenses we will use as we read the letter. These two chapters will include exploration of some sections of the letter that illuminate the problem in the Galatians churches. Consider reading the whole letter before starting chapter one of this commentary.

In chapter three we begin working our way through the whole letter. Chapters three through twelve are each divided into five parts. First, is **The Text** of the section of Galatians that the chapter will explore, from the New International Version (2011). Second, **The Flow and Form of the Text** part of the chapter will identify the literary form of the passage and situate it in the larger context of the letter. Third, **The Text Explained** guides the reader through the section, not necessarily discussing each verse but giving significant insights about the text. It focuses on the meaning for the original recipients of the letter. The purpose is not to lay out various possible interpretations or to summarize scholarly debate but to give a coherent sense of the meaning of the section. Scholarly jargon and footnotes are avoided. Greek words are occasionally discussed when they add nuance of understanding or are crucial for interpreting the text. Based on the previous sections, the fourth section builds bridges to our time and explores **Implications of the Text for Today**. Finally, the **Personal Reflection Questions** connect the content of the chapter, and most specifically the implications section, to your life and the life of your church community. The questions will invite further reflection and application. Some are more individual in nature; most are intended to provide the basis for group discussion after personal reflection.

At a number of places in the book I explain in more depth a **Significant Concept**. These concepts are crucial in the interpretation of the whole letter, not just for understanding a particular verse or section. Therefore, I will refer to these concepts repeatedly throughout the book. I have listed them in the table of contents to make it easier for you to refer back to the explanations.

Within the text of the book I will occasionally point you to something you could read to explore a topic in more depth. I also will quote other authors at times, and at the end of the quote or the end of the author's idea I will place the author's last name, date of publication, and page reference, like: (Barclay 2016, 1). You can find the title and full reference of the article or book in the **References** at the end of the book.

CHAPTER ONE

The Picture Paul Had in Mind

Paul's letter to the churches in Galatia overflows with passion. He is upset and it shows (1:6; 3:1; 5:12). What has provoked him to write this impassioned letter? We will seek to answer that question in these first two chapters.

Some Christians in Galatia were concerned about tensions and confusion in the churches. They sent a messenger to Paul, perhaps with a letter, who informed him about the situation. Paul discussed the situation with the messenger in order to more fully understand it and then wrote a letter in response. We have Paul's letter, but we do not have the report he received. In order to make sense of his response, we must have a picture in our mind of the situation he is addressing. It is hard to explain a solution without talking about the problem.

Imagine yourself in the same room as someone involved in a phone conversation. You are interested, you want to know what is going on, but you hear only half the conversation. What do you do? You try to reconstruct what the person on the other end is saying based on what you can hear. Similarly, in order to get a picture of the issues in Galatia that Paul had in mind when he wrote, we do best by looking at the letter for clues. Unfortunately, for the last 500 years many readers of Galatians have not done that. They have looked elsewhere for a picture of the problems that prompted Paul's letter to the Galatians.

Out of fairness to those who have done this, myself included, it is not so much that we went looking for clues in the wrong place. Rather, we received and accepted a picture of the problem without asking if it matched up with the letter itself.

I will first describe this picture that comes from outside the letter and suggest why it became so influential. Then I will propose an alternative picture for us to have in mind as we read the letter —a picture from within the letter itself.

Picture of the Problem in Galatia, Possibility #1: Individuals Burdened by Guilt Seeking Peace through Works

What was the image Paul had in mind as he dictated his letter to the Galatians? Many assume he pictured individuals seeking release from guilt through doing good works. Yet, finding that no matter how many works they did or religious rituals they performed, they did not experience peace with God or freedom from the weight of guilt. With this image in mind, people assume Paul wrote Galatians to correct an erroneous teaching that salvation is achieved through good works and to proclaim the opposite: that salvation is by God's grace through faith. Although there are some connections between Paul's letter and this picture—for instance, talk in the letter of justification by faith, not by works—there is a major problem. The word "guilt" does not appear even once in the whole letter. If this is the heart of the problem Paul had in mind, wouldn't he have mentioned it?

This commonly assumed picture comes not from clues in the letter but from a very influential reader of Paul—the key figure in the Protestant Reformation. It is a picture of Martin Luther's experience. He lived in a time when there was a significant amount of erroneous teaching on the relationship of works and salvation. Luther sought to ease his guilt through human efforts. Yet even becoming a disciplined and dedicated monk did not bring him peace with God or freedom from his feelings of guilt. Then, through reading Galatians and Romans, Luther experienced release. He understood, and experienced, that peace with God is a gift received by faith, not achieved by works. Luther then passionately proclaimed this liberating good news to others like himself. He wrote about, preached, and taught what he had experienced—that Paul's writings corrected a mistaken concept of salvation. Luther's experience and interpretation of Paul has shaped the way many read Galatians today, even those who have never actually read anything Luther wrote on Paul.

Was Luther correct? His liberation from guilt by experiencing God's grace through reading Galatians and Romans was authentic and appropriate. It was not a mistake to apply Galatians to his life in this way nor was it a mistake to use it to correct erroneous teachings about salvation through human efforts. I fully affirm that God's Spirit spoke to Luther through Paul's writing and guided Luther in his proclamation of what he experienced. In that sense, yes, Luther was correct.

Was Luther's situation what Paul had in mind when he wrote the letter? No, it was not. So how can I affirm Luther's experience as correct and also say his experience is not the right picture for Galatians? Another analogy offers help here. I am a professor. I often read books or listen to lectures by other professors. I am the audience they have in mind. I learn from them and use their ideas in my teaching. I also get input from people in other professions. I remember attending a leadership conference. The auditorium was filled with pastors and ministry leaders. The speakers directed their talk at leaders—not at professors like me. Much of it did not apply to me. Yet at various moments a story or comment sparked ideas I could use in my teaching. I connected their talk with my world. But the fact that I got a great insight for teaching does not mean they had professors like me in mind when they prepared their talk, or even that they were trying to communicate the insight I received.

Luther did something like that. He connected with Paul's writing and applied it to his situation. Like me at that leadership conference, he got some great things from Paul. And just as the speakers at the conference communicated much more to their intended audience of ministry leaders than I took from their talks, so Paul communicated much more to his intended audience than Luther took from the letters. I recommend that we set aside this first picture, not because it produces insights from Galatians that are incorrect, but because it is too limited. Instead of rooting our interpretation of Galatians in Luther's experience in 16th century Germany, let us seek to root it in Paul's experience. A different picture will enable us to get so much more out of Galatians. Let us go back, as it were, and listen to the original phone call.

Picture of the Problem in Galatia, Possibility #2: Religious-Cultural Dividing Lines Split a Church (Gal 2:11-14)

What if during that phone call, the person you can hear suddenly says, "That reminds me of a story," and then starts telling the story.

What a great clue! You still would not know what the other person had said, but you would know it was similar to the story you are listening to. We can do the same thing with Paul. He recounts to the Galatians an experience he had at the church in Antioch. He includes in the story some theological statements he applies to the situation in Galatia. He clearly saw a connection between what had happened earlier in Antioch and what was happening in Galatia.

In Galatians 2:11-14, Paul recalls a beautiful scene of Jewish and Gentile Christians eating together in Antioch; those whom culture and religion have separated are united in Christ. The table fellowship they share offers a concrete example of people becoming a new creation through the cross of Jesus Christ (6:15-16). To appreciate the radical nature of this table fellowship more fully, we must recognize the role of the table in the first-century biblical context.

In most cultures, the people you eat with matters. If someone invites you to share a meal, they are communicating something by that act. In some cultures, including the biblical world of the first century, the significance was much greater. To invite someone to share a meal communicated acceptance and honor. It was not done casually. In the world of Jesus, Peter, and Paul, the Jews used the dinner table, along with circumcision and Sabbath observance, to foster unity amongst their people and create a sense of distinction from non-Jews. By excluding non-Jews from the table, Jews could maintain their distinctive religious and cultural identity.

However, God uses a dream about food to lead Peter to begin the work of breaking down this barrier and to preach the gospel to Gentiles (Acts 10:10-48). Therefore, it should not surprise us when Peter visits the church in Antioch and comfortably takes his place at the table to share the meal with the other followers of Jesus—both Gentiles and Jews (2:12).

Yet tragically, the beautiful image of one united table of fellowship does not last. Some Jewish Christians arrive from Jerusalem, the mother church. Unable to overcome years of drawing lines of separation through their actions, they cannot eat with Gentiles. Instead, they sit at a separate table. Whether through explicit statements or the nonverbal implication of dining at a separate table, these emissaries from the Jerusalem church draw a line that communicates to the Gentile Christians that they are inferior. They can leave the inferior group and join the Jews at the table *only* if they become circumcised and follow other traditional Jewish laws.

Imagine the shame and abandonment that the Gentile Christians must have felt when the local Jewish Christians, who had previously eaten with them, left the table of union to join the newly arrived visitors at the Jewish-only table in the corner. They not only stopped eating with the Gentile Christians, they also ceased celebrating the Lord's Supper together. In the early church, communion was most likely not a separate event but part of the shared meal.

Paul tells us that Peter is afraid of those who are pressuring the Gentile Christians to become circumcised (2:12). Afraid of what? Before we imagine the scene, I invite you to remember a time when you felt that others were looking at you as if you were on the wrong side of a religious line. Now imagine what Peter might have thought and felt as he sat at the table with the Gentiles and the disbelieving stares of the Jerusalem emissaries penetrated into his being. He might have imagined them going back to the church in Jerusalem, saying, "You will not believe what Peter is doing in Antioch!" Under the scrutiny of their shaming gaze, Peter moves to the other table. Now, imagine that you are another Jewish Christian who is still sitting at the table with Gentiles. You are not renowned like Peter. Perhaps you are a new follower of Jesus. You see Peter, one of the twelve disciples of Jesus, leave. If *he* no longer thinks it is appropriate to eat at a table with Gentiles, how can *you* stay? Sadly, almost all the Jewish Christians—even Barnabas—leave the unified table (2:13). Only one Jewish Christian—Paul—remains at the table with the Gentile Christians. What a tragedy, from new creation unity to division along religious and cultural lines.

What picture did Paul have in mind when he wrote this letter? We can't know for sure—remember we only are hearing one side of the telephone call—but we can be almost certain that part of what he had in mind was this scene in Antioch. He pictured something similar happening in Galatia and wrote his impassioned letter seeking to prevent the church communities in Galatia splitting apart. To get a more complete sense of the problem in Galatia we will need to look at other clues in the letter. We will work at that in the next chapter. The rest of this chapter will provide two tools that will help us better understand the incident at Antioch and aid our interpretation of the rest of the letter.

Interpretive Lens: Honor-Shame Dynamic

Think back to your high school days. What group were you in? What group did you want to be in? Can you recall a time when you did not wear the right clothes or did or said the wrong thing? Or, perhaps a time when you, or your whole group, were excluded or looked down upon by another group? In those moments you likely felt shame.

How about the opposite? Can you recall a time you felt not just "in," but a strong sense of others approving of what you had done, what you were wearing, or what you said? You probably did not use the word "honor," but that is what your peers did. They honored you. We could say that what the group affirmed is what it considered honorable. If you made a list of behaviors that were encouraged or discouraged, that would be the group's honor code. All societies have some expressions of an honor-shame dynamic, others are saturated with honor-shame dynamics. That was the case in the cultures we find in the Bible.

What do people most strive for? Think about that question in relation to society in general in your context. Another way of asking the question is, what motivates their actions? Wealth, pleasure, power, fame are common things people most desire in North America today. In the world of the Roman Empire in Paul's time, people most desired honor. They wanted their neighbors to think highly of them. In contemporary North America one can achieve status through wealth. Think of how we publish lists of the richest individuals, or report someone's net worth—the more wealth, the more status. That was not the case in the first century Mediterranean world. Wealth by itself did not give someone high status. People measured the amount of honor someone had acquired, not their net worth. People desired wealth, but it was so they could use money to take actions to gain honor.

For instance, people could gain honor by using their wealth to host a meal. People recognized the act itself as honorable, but there were layers of honor accrual going on at meals. As I noted already, table fellowship had a heightened sense of communicating honor and acceptance in the time of Jesus and Paul. The person who hosted the meal honored people with an invitation, and they honored the host by accepting (or dishonored the host by refusing). The host invited people of as high status as possible, but not too high because that carried the risk of the shame of a refused invitation. The higher the status of the people attending a meal the more honor gained by the host—not only because of honoring the host by sitting at table with him, but also because those who came to the meal would be expected to return the invitation. It was the honorable thing to do. Therefore another way one accrued honor through a meal was through the honor of being invited to other meals by people of status. And, as we see in Luke 14:7-11, the honor game also played out in the seating arrangements at a meal.

Seeking honor and avoiding shame was central, not just in table fellowship, but in shaping people's actions, large and small. As Cicero wrote, "life was lived under the constant, withering gaze of opinion, everyone constantly reckoning up the honour of others" (Lendon 1997, 36). People gained honor through acting virtuously, giving gifts that benefitted the community, being faithful to a patron or friend, acts of valor, etc. People also had ascribed honor, high or low, which they were born with, based on things like class, citizenship, ethnic group, family of origin, or whether they were slave or free. Although I have given examples of individual honor, in the New Testament world honor was as much or more communal. First, an individual's action brought honor and shame not just for themselves, but for their family and other social groups to which they belonged. Second, not just individuals acted to seek honor. Groups, cities, and nations did as well. So, in thinking about Galatians, we should look not just for critique of self-righteousness, but of group-righteousness.

Obtaining honor was competitive. It depended on comparison with others. Honor was a precious, unstable, and limited good. For one group or person to gain honor, another one lost honor. John Barclay notes, "almost all social relations in Paul's Roman context were both ordered and threatened by the competition for honor. In the absence of 'objective' measures of quality, a person's worth was heavily dependent on his or her public reputation, a 'dignity' energetically claimed and fiercely defended" (Barclay 2014, 311).

What do we see if we look at the table scene in Antioch (2:11-14) through the lens of an honor seeking society? First, we recognize that people in that setting would have had great sensitivity about who they were eating with and how it would impact their reputation and the reputation of that group. Second, it helps us recognize ethnic dynamics playing out. Jewish people might have lost honor among other groups for being out of the religious mainstream of the time, but their self-perception was of having high honor as the chosen people of the one God. They saw themselves as more honorable than Gentiles. Therefore, to keep that honor it was very important for them to maintain their right standing with God and to maintain their distinctness from other peoples. As we will explore later in the book, key ways of doing this were circumcision, sabbath observance, and table practices. Thus through the lens of an honor-seeking society we better understand some of the dynamics driving the actions of the Jewish Christians from Jerusalem who refused to eat with Gentile Christians. We also have a greater sense of how radical it was that Christians in Antioch had been coming together at one table. They ignored common honor categories and calculations. They followed a new honor code. For them the honorable thing was to pull down the barriers of status separation.

Another important aspect of this lens is the way an honor-shame orientation contrasts with the guilt-innocence orientation we observed in the Luther picture above. All cultures have means for influencing people to behave in ways that culture considers appropriate. Those cultures with a stronger honor-shame orientation lean more heavily on a public verdict. The pressure of the opinion of others shapes behavior. People seek to do things others consider honorable and avoid doing things others consider shameful. If someone does what is dishonorable that person loses face before others. In contrast, cultures with a stronger innocence-guilt orientation lean more heavily on an internal verdict. These cultures seek to internalize within people the values and standards of the society and shape individuals to feel guilty if they transgress.

Contrasting guilt and shame clarifies the meaning of each. Guilt is an internal sense of moral failure and is felt even if no one else knows about the transgression. In contrast, shame is a sense of unworthiness. It is integrally connected to exposure before peers or those in authority in a social network and produces feelings of humiliation, rejection, disapproval, loss of status, and abandonment. It can be experienced as actual expulsion from a group.

Guilt is resolved through punishment, restitution, pardon or forgiveness, or a combination of them. In contrast, since shame is relational, release from shame must be relational. The remedy for shame includes removing disgrace, receiving a new identity, restoring honor, and overcoming exclusion through reincorporation.

In most cultures, people experience both guilt and shame. It is not the absence of guilt or internalized ideas about right and wrong that leads us to label Galatia, and the New Testament world, an honor-shame culture. Rather, it is that the honor-shame orientation was dominant. To say the honor-shame dynamic was dominant in the Roman Empire means all groups used honor and shame as means to shape behavior. It does not, however, mean they had the same definition of what was honorable. As noted above, Jews had a distinctly different perspective on what was honorable than other groups and religions in the Empire. Like their neighbors they used shame and honor to shape behavior, but very different behaviors.

We will use the lens of honor-shame throughout our interpretation of the letter. I will use the term "honor," but also other terms more common in Western cultures that relate to the honor dynamic explained in this section—terms such as "dignity" and "status." The honor-shame lens has already helped us understand dynamics of the divided table at Antioch. Awareness of the dominance of an honor-shame orientation in that time reinforces the conclusion that possibility #2—religious-cultural dividing lines split a church—is the better option. An individual struggling with a burden of guilt is not likely the picture Paul had in mind as he wrote the letter. More likely, he imagined people burdened with shame.

For a more in-depth description of the honor-shame dynamic and examples of it in the Bible I recommend reading the first five chapters of a book I co-authored with Jayson Georges, *Ministering in Honor-Shame Cultures: Biblical Foundations and Practical Essentials*. To get a feel of just how much honor and shame pervaded life in the New Testament world I recommend reading one of these novels, written by scholars of the New Testament: *The Lost Letters of Pergamum: A Story from the New Testament World* by Bruce Longenecker, or *A Week in the Life of Rome* by James Papandrea.

Interpretive Lens: Bounded, Fuzzy, and Centered Churches

Paul Hiebert, a Mennonite Brethren missionary in India, asked the question: when is someone considered a Christian? Previously, he said, he had a clear answer to that question, but it did not function in India. Hiebert used an example from India of a man named Papayya. Should he be considered a Christian after he hears a story about Jesus and salvation through the cross and says a prayer expressing his desire to worship Jesus with other Christians? What if Papayya refers to Jesus as God, or the son of God, but uses a word for "God" that has a significantly different meaning than the English, Hebrew, or Greek terms for God? What if Papayya offers incense to a picture of Jesus on the shelf in his home, but does not take the other gods off the shelf? What if he starts attending church, but still participates in Hindu celebrations? When should Papayya be considered a Christian?

Exploring this question further in his work, Hiebert argues that the way people conceptualize church and the category of Christian will shape how they answer the question about Papayya. Hiebert, a cultural anthropologist, borrows from mathematical set theory to describe three different ways to categorize people (Hiebert 1978; 1994, 107–36). These will provide an excellent aid in understanding Paul's letter to the Galatians.

Bounded Sets

Hiebert explains that bounded sets have a clear, static boundary line that allows for a uniform definition of those who are within the group. In general terms, a bounded group creates a list of essential characteristics that determine whether or not a person belongs to that group. For example, a league soccer team is a bounded group. There are try-outs. Ability matters. A team also has other requirements, such as having a uniform, attending practices, paying dues to the league, and so on. Coaches draw a

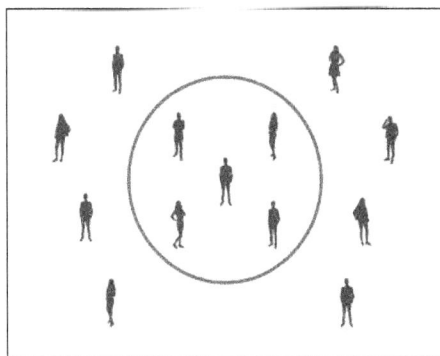

clear line to determine which players have the ability and meet the requirements to be on the team. Their uniforms identify them as belonging to the same team. As the diagram illustrates, everyone who is not part of the team is on the other side of the line.

BOUNDED SETS

Fuzzy Sets

A fuzzy set is similar to a bounded set, but the boundary line is removed—or at least less clear. The grounds for distinction are rather vague, and so the group is fuzzy. Imagine a city park where people gather on Sunday afternoons to play pickup games. The same people might participate week after week, but someone could miss several weeks and still show up and play. If others think you are a lousy player you might have a hard time getting on a pickup team, but they would not tell you the criteria for making that decision. Some people might play soccer each time they go to the park, while others might play ultimate frisbee. One week you might show up and find volleyball nets taking up the whole field. As the following diagram illustrates, group membership cannot be clearly established.

Though bounded and fuzzy groups differ radically, they share the same paradigm about how to define who belongs to a group, though they are positioned at opposite ends of a continuum. At one end, the boundary line is clear; near the other end the line gets increasingly vague and then totally disappears.

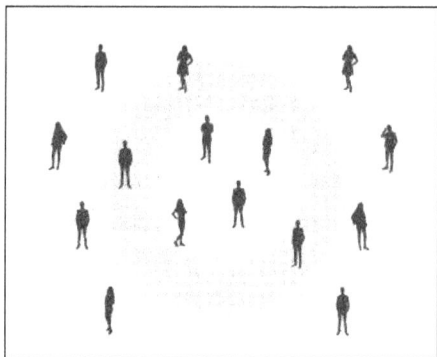

FUZZY SETS

Centered Sets

A centered set reflects a completely different paradigm. This third-way option is not on the bounded-fuzzy continuum. Rather than drawing a line to identify people based on their common characteristics, a centered set uses a directional and relational basis of evaluation. The group is created by defining a center and observing people's relationship with the center. As the following diagram illustrates, the set is made up of all who are oriented toward the center.

Hiebert says that even though some people may be far from the center, they are part of the centered group if they are heading toward the center. On the other hand, some people may be close to the center, but they are not part of the centered group because they have turned around and are moving away from it. Though the people within a centered group may not be uniform in their characteristics, they will all be heading the same direction.

In the soccer example, a centered approach would be when someone invites anyone who wants to play soccer to gather at a local public park on Saturday afternoon at three o'clock. In the diagram, those who show up are represented by the people whose arrows are heading toward the defined center, which is soccer. Those who do not show up to play are represented by the people whose arrows are turned away from the center. Some of those who show up may not be very good, but their lack of ability will not exclude them, because the invitation is open to all who want to play. If too many people show up, the organizers will start another game. The group will not define who can play or cannot play based on ability or who can afford the fees.

After describing these three approaches to group membership, Hiebert applies the model to churches.

CENTERED SETS

Bounded Churches

Bounded churches draw a line that distinguishes insiders from outsiders, Christians from non-Christians, or true Christians from mediocre Christians. The line generally consists of a list of correct beliefs and certain visible behaviors. In the Antioch incident the visitors from Jerusalem display a bounded group approach by asking questions such as, "Have you been circumcised? Are you following Jewish sabbath laws?" In essence they have drawn a line and anyone who is not an observant Jew or not living like a Jew is seen as being on the other side of the line.

What churches come to mind when you read the previous paragraph? Many of us might think of legalistic churches. While legalism does provide a clear example of a bounded approach, boundedness is not limited to legalism. In fact, I have participated in churches that were self-righteously *not* legalistic, where we looked with disdain on legalistic Christians in the same way that they might have looked with contempt on those who fell short of their standards. Though we had radically different lines, we all drew lines in a bounded-set way. Bounded churches can use a variety of things to draw lines that define insiders from outsiders, including rituals, spiritual experiences, political commitments, activism, attendance, beliefs, and behaviors.

In critiquing a bounded approach to church, I am not critiquing any and all things that we might call boundaries. The problem is not with having a line that differentiates between things that are acceptable and unacceptable, but with how bounded churches use those lines to separate and categorize people in a judgmental way.

The boundary lines drawn by bounded churches enable those on the inside to gain status and feel superior to those who do not meet the standards. While many people appreciate the clarity of a bounded church and the security it offers, the boundary lines injure both those who are excluded and the insiders who exclude. The boundary lines hinder transparency because members find it difficult to express their struggles honestly when they are afraid of losing their standing in the church. Outsiders experience the pain of not fitting in while insiders sacrifice their distinct and complex individualities in order to belong. Bounded churches use the threat of shame as motivation to stay within the line. For instance, shame courses through the scene of the divided tables in Antioch. Peter felt it in the disbelieving stares of the emissaries from Jerusalem, which penetrated into his being, so he sought to avoid further shame by leaving the united table and joining the Jews. But the Gentile Christians could not go to that table because they were on the wrong side of the line; they were excluded and felt shamed. Bounded churches are characterized by unity based on uniformity, strict but often superficial ethics, conditional acceptance, shame, fear, lack of transparency, and self-righteousness (Baker 1999, 17–33).

Fuzzy Churches

Some churches recognize the problematic fruit of line drawing within bounded churches and opt for what appears to be the obvious solution: they erase the line. This fuzzy approach to church comes naturally in many places today. In a relativistic society that holds tolerance as the supreme virtue, a bounded church is problematic, whereas a fuzzy church is not. Yet fuzzy churches solve one set of problems while creating others. A fuzzy approach produces churches that are less defined, less cohesive, and more relativistic. Rather than passionately dialoguing to clarify the truth, fuzzy churches focus on tolerance. I have observed "whateverism" in fuzzy churches not only when people refrain from confronting others about sinful actions, but also in their hesitancy to describe certain actions or beliefs as inappropriate. In a fuzzy church, people are reluctant to talk about the need for personal transformation, let alone conversion, because it feels "intolerant" to call someone to repent, and the boundary lines are so fuzzy there is no basis for repentance.

Centered Churches

Unlike fuzzy churches, centered churches can distinguish who belongs to the group from who does not. In a centered church, God is the center focus. Therefore, the critical question is, *to whom do we offer our worship and allegiance?* Two types of change happen in a centered church. The first is directional. Is someone facing the center or oriented in the other direction? From this perspective, conversion happens when someone turns toward the center. The second change relates to distance—moving closer to or further away from the center. Such movement varies because members do not move at the same pace. The group is *unified* by the first change because they are all oriented toward Jesus Christ. However, they are not *uniform* because the characteristics of the various members will differ due to their varying distances from the center.

The centered paradigm facilitates sincere and deep relationship because unity does not come from uniformity, but from a common orientation toward the center. There is space to struggle and fail because everyone recognizes they are in process—that is, moving closer to the center.

A bounded church focuses on defining and maintaining the boundary, whereas a centered church focuses on defining the center and maintaining clarity about the church's center, which is, first and foremost, Jesus Christ—not only in terms of our beliefs about Jesus, but more importantly who Jesus is, how Jesus reveals God, and how the Spirit of Jesus remains alive and present today. The center is further defined by the Bible, the gospel, and theological traditions that have shaped the community.

By discerning group membership through people's trajectories and their relationship to the center, a centered church remedies the problems that motivate a fuzzy church to blur boundaries while also avoiding the negative fruit that grows out of a fuzzy approach. A centered church has a greater sense of welcome and inclusion than a bounded church because its identity does not depend on excluding others. There is much more space for people to explore and to participate in the life of the church while considering their relationship with the center. Yet, it is not the "everyone is in" of a fuzzy church. The orientation of one's arrow matters. If one is not oriented toward the center, one is not part of the group. The centered paradigm provides the possibility of conversion and repentance, articulates what is right and wrong, establishes a standard (the center), and calls people to a different way of living.

A more in-depth explanation, with real-life examples, of these three categories is available in a video series I made at centeredsetchurch.com, or in the introduction and first three chapters of my book *Centered-Set Church: Discipleship and Community Without Judgmentalism.*

Hiebert's concepts of bounded, fuzzy, and centered are new, but what he labels bounded-set dynamics were very much part of the honor-shame culture that Paul and the Galatians lived in. Societal and religious lines defined acceptable behavior. People sought to save face by staying on the right side of the lines. They constantly sought out markers that would define them as honorable.

Paul does not use terminology of bounded, fuzzy, and centered sets in his letter, but the dynamics described above are there.

Looking at the letter through the lens of these concepts will aid in our understanding of it. And through the letter we will grow in our understanding of what is a centered church.

Now, having affirmed that when Paul wrote the letter he more likely had in mind the image of the divided church in Antioch than a guilt-burdened individual confused about works and grace, and having two helpful interpretive lenses, we will next look at the letter as a whole for clues to answer the question: What has provoked Paul to write this impassioned letter? Before continuing, I recommend you read Galatians again for hints about the problems in the Galatian churches.

Personal Response

- In what ways has picture #1, the Luther-shaped image, influenced how you have read and understood Galatians and Romans?

- How do you respond to the idea of looking within the letter itself to find the picture Paul had in mind?

- How do you imagine the second picture, the religious-cultural division at Antioch, might lead to a different reading of Galatians than the first picture?

- How have you seen or experienced each of Hiebert's three categories? How does your experience match with the fruits of each category described above?

CHAPTER TWO

The Problem in Galatia

Who Paul is Writing To?

An important step in reconstructing the situation Paul is responding to when writing this letter is identifying to whom he is writing.
We know a few things directly from the letter. Paul knew the
people he wrote to. They were his spiritual children (4:19). When
he was with them, preaching and starting these churches he was
recuperating from a sickness (4:13). They believed, received the
Holy Spirit, and God did miracles among them (3:1-5; 4:13-15). A
key piece of information, that relates to the story from Antioch,
is that the people in the Galatian churches he wrote to were
predominantly, or perhaps totally, Gentiles (4:8).

Paul states explicitly that he is writing to the churches of Galatia
(1:2) and addresses them as "Galatians" (3:1). On the surface it
appears there is no mystery about the audience. In actuality,
however, we do not know for sure where these churches were. A

region in northern Asia Minor was called Galatia because ethnic Galatians lived there, but Rome organized a province with the name Galatia that included other areas further south, including Iconium, Lystra, and Derbe. We know Paul visited the latter places (Acts 14:1-23), and Acts also mentions him passing through Galatia, but we do not know if that refers to the northern region or the whole province (Acts 16:6; 18:23). Paul could be referring to churches in the north, the south, or both. We also do not know how many churches he wrote to, nor when he wrote the letter—probably sometime in the 50s A.D. Although some scholars have invested significant energy researching and debating these matters, they do not have a significant impact on interpretation of the letter.

The Other Missionaries

From reading Galatians we can see clearly that a group of people were, from Paul's perspective, instigating problems in the churches. Therefore, piecing together information about them will also help us understand what Paul is so upset about.

Paul mentions these other missionaries various times in the letter (1:6-9; 3:1-2, 5; 4:17; 5:7-12; 6:12-14). Throughout the letter Paul uses "you" to refer to the Galatians and "they" to refer to the missionaries. Therefore, we know they are not members of the Galatian churches. They may have come from Jerusalem, but we do not know. They identified themselves as followers of Jesus Christ. It appears they were Jewish Christians, not just because they put so much emphasis on Jewish laws and traditions, but also because they had been circumcised (6:13). Paul called them agitators who sowed confusion (1:7; 5:12). I will frequently use Paul's term and call them agitators. But I have chosen "other missionaries" as their primary label. Paul was a missionary who had first evangelized and taught in Galatia. Now other missionaries had arrived. They would not have called themselves agitators. They probably would have considered themselves, like Paul, as teachers or missionaries—preachers of the gospel. Immediately putting them in the category of bad agitators makes it too easy to think of ourselves as very different from them. The more we can recognize similarities we might have with them, the more we will get out of Galatians.

There is nothing in the letter that implies these other missionaries denied that Jesus was the Messiah through whom God had acted to provide salvation. In addition to that affirmation, it appears they taught that to truly be part of the People of God, full participants in the covenant, it was necessary to live like a Jew. From all the talk of circumcision and law in the letter, we conclude that they told the Gentile Christians in the Galatian churches that the men needed to become circumcised and that they all needed to obey God's commandments and practice key traditions that distinguished Jews from pagans. From what Paul says about Abraham in the letter we can guess that the agitators probably preached that to receive the full blessings promised to Abraham they had to follow his example and be circumcised. In sum, to be true Christians, the Galatian Christian communities needed to live like Jews. Whether they stated it explicitly or not, the agitators treated the Galatian Christians as if they were not fully converted.

We do not know their motives, but it is easy to imagine they had a sincere desire to honor God's word and were driven by evangelistic zeal to proclaim what they viewed as a fuller version of the gospel. Desires for peace and less persecution may have motivated them as well. These missionaries had either been persecuted or feared persecution (6:12). Our honor-shame interpretive lens leads us to ask how the Gentile Christians might be causing these teachers, and other Jewish Christians, to lose honor. Others in the Roman Empire scorned and ridiculed Christians for being in a movement that, unlike other religions, was new and lacked formal rites, rituals, and temples. Heightening the connection with Jewish traditions, a well-established and recognized religion, could lessen those shaming voices. From another direction, other Jews were scandalized by Jewish Christians mixing with Gentiles the way Paul, Peter, and others did at Antioch. Therefore, if Gentile Christians would adopt Jewish ways it would lessen the pressure from both sides. They may have even presented this as a way to facilitate other Jews following Jesus, and also increase evangelistic possibilities with Gentiles by more strongly linking the way of Jesus with an ancient religion.

This portrait of the other missionaries further reinforces that, rather than the picture of an individual burdened by guilt, the picture of the divided table at Antioch is the better one to have in mind as we interpret the letter. Concerns for the community drove both Paul and the other missionaries. Neither was focused on the question of individuals burdened by guilt. The central questions were what defines the Christian community and who can sit at the table and celebrate the Lord's Supper together.

Stereotype of the Other Missionaries

Martin Luther experienced an explicit teaching of works earning salvation, or in the case of selling indulgences, buying salvation. Therefore, through the lens of Luther's experience many have seen these missionaries paralleling those distorting the gospel at the time of Luther. This led to an interpretation that the problem in Galatia was a false teaching of salvation by works, and Paul responded to the problem by confronting works righteousness and proclaiming salvation by grace. The characterization of the other missionaries as teaching salvation by works is rooted in a caricature of Jews explicitly teaching that salvation was gained through obeying the law. In the last few decades numerous New Testament scholars have countered that this is an inaccurate stereotype.

These scholars carefully read Jewish documents from that time period. These writings stated that salvation was always by God's gracious initiative. Jews of Paul's time understood that God gave the law in the context of the covenant. The law did not provide a means to achieve fellowship with God. God had already taken the initiative and done that. The law showed Israel how to live in covenant with God, and made it possible to do so by providing a system of atonement for when they sinned and fell short. Obedience to the law was not taught as a means to earn salvation, but as that which kept one within the covenant (Sanders 1977, 180, 419–28). These scholars concluded that if Jews did not teach that salvation was earned through merit-accumulating works, then it is incorrect to say that in Galatians Paul attacks such a teaching. How could Paul attack a teaching that did not exist?*

I accept the argument that the Jewish texts did not teach merit-based salvation, and therefore I also accept that Paul, in

---

* What is described in this paragraph is an aspect of what is called the "New Perspective." It is fairly common today to divide scholars of Paul into "New Perspective" and "Traditional" (referring to traditional post-Reformation Protestant interpretation of Paul). In this commentary I will not use the label "New Perspective" because in reality there are various new perspectives. There are significant differences between those commonly put in the New Perspective category. Therefore, I will focus on particular interpretive issues without seeking to identify them as belonging to one position or another. I also do not identify myself with either "camp." With the New Perspective position I affirm that Paul wrote with deep concern for the communal character of the churches; with the traditionalist position I affirm that Paul, in confronting works righteousness, emphasized the centrality of God's grace.

Galatians and other places, was not attacking an explicit teaching of salvation by works. But to say that Paul did not confront a *teaching* of salvation by works does not necessarily mean he did not confront a lived out works righteousness. Let me repeat these important points. I affirm that the other missionaries did not teach that salvation was by works, and I affirm that Paul in Galatians confronted a problem of works righteousness.

To understand how this apparently contradictory statement is not a contradiction, let us reflect on bounded churches for a moment. All the bounded churches that I have participated in have clearly taught that salvation is by grace and not by works. Yet many people in the churches lived as if their salvation, their acceptance by God, and inclusion within the people of God, depended on their staying on the right side of the boundary line. This contradiction between what was stated and what was lived or perceived is even more pronounced if we observe what bounded churches communicate to outsiders.

For example, after a Honduran woman told me she had visited a church the night before, she said, "I almost accepted Jesus Christ last night." When I asked her why she had not, she explained that she could not accept Jesus because she was a sinner. Rather than seeking God's forgiveness because she was a sinner, this woman had learned from her observations of churches and Christians that in order to accept Jesus, she had to comply with the rules of the church first. Because this woman could not marry her common-law husband for a variety of reasons, she could not cross to the right side of the line. Although she wanted to, the lines drawn led her to think she could not become a Christian. Sadly, she was not alone in this misconception. While doing research on bounded churches in Tegucigalpa, Honduras, I interviewed both church members and people who do not attend church (Baker 1999, 1–33,

49–55). One of the questions I asked non-believers was, "According to the evangelical church, what do you have to do to become a Christian?" Most commonly articulated, especially by those who had contact with churches, was a works-oriented salvation. They said something like: "get your life in order and then you can become a Christian." The churches' line-drawing had communicated more loudly than their statements about God's grace.

Returning to the table drama in Antioch can help us imagine how something similar might have been occurring there and in the Galatian churches. The visitors were from the Jerusalem church. People in that church had known Jesus personally. Clearly that church would have preached salvation by grace through trusting in Jesus. In recounting the story, Paul says nothing about the visitors or Peter teaching erroneous doctrine. The focus is on their actions. Imagine yourself as one of the Gentile Christians at Antioch. What would these Christians from Jerusalem have communicated by refusing to eat with you? Might it make you feel like you had not done enough? Would you feel there was something else you needed to do to truly be a Christian, even if they did not say anything about living like them being required for salvation? In a bounded church, the sermon is not the only thing that communicates; the line of division communicates as well. The bounded character of the churches I observed in Honduras spoke louder than their words. I believe the same thing happened in Antioch and was happening in Galatia. Paul confronted a works righteousness that flowed not from explicit statements that salvation was through human effort, but from the bounded attitude and line-drawing practices of these Jewish Christian missionaries.

As I previously stated: the other missionaries did not teach that salvation was by works, yet Paul in Galatians confronted a problem of works righteousness. Affirming both parts of this sentence opens possibilities for reading of Galatians with deeper meaning and greater impact on our lives. To picture the other missionaries as teaching that salvation is by works too easily leads those of us who preach salvation is by grace to view ourselves as "right," and to see Galatians as a corrective for others. I acknowledge having this view in the past when I led Bible studies on Galatians to help people confused about grace and works. It was for them, not for me.

To affirm the first statement invites us to re-evaluate how much we might have in common with the visiting missionaries in Galatia. It keeps me from simply viewing Galatians as important text for others, but not for me. The second statement forces us to go deeper in our reading of the letter. Having a correct articulation of salvation by grace did not protect the other missionaries and does not automatically protect us from living as if acceptance by God and others is based on works. There is more going on in Galatians than an argument over doctrinal articulation. There is something deeper and more powerful. Where did the works righteousness, and the judgmentalism and shame that accompanies it, come from if not from explicit teaching about salvation by human effort? We began answering that question by pointing to the impact of bounded group line-drawing in Antioch. The next section will take us a layer deeper.

Let us first review what we can say at this point in regards to the questions: Why is Paul so upset? What has provoked him to write this letter? Paul is upset by the other missionaries' emphasis on the necessity of Jewish practices which are causing confusion about the gospel, shaming Gentile Christians, and threatening to tear apart the church communities of Galatia.

Religion

If the root problem in Galatia was simply incorrect doctrinal teaching, Paul would have just provided a correct alternative statement. If the root problem in Galatia was simply mistaken standards for who can join together at the table, he would have offered other requirements instead of circumcision. He does not. Clearly doctrinal teaching and ethical standards are important and both are in the letter. But Paul takes us deeper. Rather than saying he is providing correction, Paul talks of liberation from enslavement (1:4; 4:3-11; 5:1). I will call this enslaving force "religion." That is not Paul's term, but using this one term will bring together a number of things he does talk about under one word. I will provide here a general explanation we will build on as we study the letter.

People use the word "religion" in different ways. My concern is not to argue that my definition is *the* right one, but it is important that you understand that in this book I will use the term in a negative way. By "religiosity" I mean our common human tendency to attempt through our efforts to gain security from God, the gods, or something that acts as a god in our lives. I am not contrasting "true religion" and "false religion." Rather, I contrast religion with biblical Christianity. Since Galatians is written about Christians and Christian communities, it might be most helpful to say I am contrasting religious Christianity with authentic Christianity.

We humans have a natural tendency to attempt to reach God or enter into a higher state through our own efforts. We seek through our actions to earn something from God or to appease God's wrath. This human religious drive is reinforced by what biblical scholar Elsa Tamez calls the world's law of merit. In day-to-day life, people's worth and standing is measured by their merits. This is true in most aspects of life—economic, social, educational, etc.

The law of merit, not the law of grace, reigns. Therefore, people naturally operate according to the law of merit in relation to God and the church as well (Tamez 1993, 130).

Jacques Ellul, French theologian and sociologist, wrote that "religion goes up and revelation comes down" (Ellul 1983, 129).

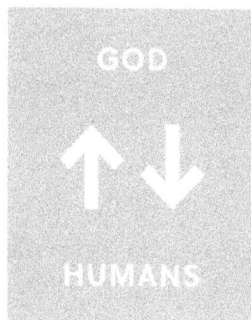

Religion perceives human action as the fundamental determinant for how God acts toward humans. Religion, as a human construct, imagines God as a god "ought" to be—powerful and high above us. The God of religion must be powerful so that it can offer the protection and security we crave. Humans imagine that this God angrily punishes misdeeds, and demands good deeds and sacrifices before acting on our behalf. The powerful accusing God of religion stands as a threatening authority behind the rules imposed by a religious system. In contrast, the fundamental heart of Christian revelation is God's gracious action toward humans. In Jesus Christ, God's loving initiative in the form of Jesus Christ literally came down to humans.

Religion is a security system. It provides security by giving us means to appease or please God. It also provides means to define who belongs to the religion and who does not, thus giving members the security of knowing they are in. Bounded group line drawing is an expression of religion. The means of claiming status that religion provides are constructed by humans. Most people would not, however, define their religion as a human invention. To do that would detract greatly from the security offered by the religion. Linking one's religion with God offers legitimacy to the lines drawn to separate the religious faithful from outsiders. Religion's perceived link with God gives it great power in people's lives.

It is correct to say that religions are human constructs, but they are more than that. I am using the term "religion" to refer to a spiritual power, one within the Pauline category of principalities and powers (Romans 8:38-3; Colossians 1:16; 2:8-10,15, 20; Ephesians 3:10; 6:12—and as we will see in the next section, Galatians 4:3-6; 8-9) (Baker 1990). As a power, it seizes and transforms our human religious drive and our human religious systems into a force that is greater than the sum of those two things. It is a force that humanly we cannot resist or control. But, as Paul boldly proclaims in Galatians, through Christ we can be liberated from the enslaving power of religion (1:4; 4:3-11; 5:1).

Religion in Galatians

I have used "religion" to refer to the root problem Paul addresses in Galatians. I have also stated that rather than impose on Galatians a description of the problem, we would look in the letter itself to reconstruct a description of the issues that provoked Paul's impassioned response. Let me point to some of the clues that what I call religion is the fundamental problem Paul addresses in Galatians.

The letter as a whole presents a contrast between a gospel rooted in God's initiative and grace and a religion rooted in human striving for status with God and other humans. The issue of religion is particularly clear in certain parts of the letter. For instance, 6:12-13 offers a picture of the teachers seeking to increase their status through success in the religious realm—the success of persuading others to follow their religious standards. It is also clear that the other missionaries are under pressure to measure up to religious standards themselves. Fear of persecution motivates their actions. Another example is the number of times that Paul emphasizes that the gospel he proclaims is not of human origin (1:1; 1:11-12; 1:16; 2:6-7). We can here say that Paul is contrasting the gospel to religion—a human construct.

Galatians 4:3-9 demonstrates most clearly that Paul sees what I have called religion as a fundamental problem in Galatia. First, referring to himself and other Jewish followers of Jesus, Paul writes:

> So also, when we were underage, we were in slavery under the elemental spiritual forces [*stoicheia*] of the world. But when the set time had fully come, God sent his Son, born of a woman, born under the law, to redeem those under the law, that we might receive adoption to sonship (4:3-5).

Note that he describes his previous experience in Judaism as enslaving. A few verses later he writes about paganism in exactly the same way. Addressing the Gentile Christians, he writes:

> Formerly, when you did not know God, you were slaves to those who by nature are not gods. But now that you know God—or rather are known by God—how is it that you are turning back to those weak and miserable forces [*stoicheia*]? Do you wish to be enslaved by them all over again? (4:8-9).

I imagine the recipients of the letter immediately wanting to protest and clarify, "No, Paul. You do not understand. We are not turning back to paganism. We are taking on practices of the people of God." But Paul is not confused. He knows that they used to practice pagan religiosity (4:8), and now as Christians they have begun to follow certain Jewish religious practices (4:10, 21; 5:2). Paul calls this turn toward following Jewish traditions a return to a previous state (4:9). How can this be? Judaism and paganism are not the same thing. Paul knows this. He does not actually say that they are returning to the same practices, but that they are returning to the same state of enslavement.

The *stoicheia* (elemental spiritual forces) enslaved Paul as a Jew. The *stoicheia* (elemental spiritual forces) enslaved Galatian Gentiles as pagans. Now, as followers of Jesus, the Galatians are at risk of being enslaved again by the *stoicheia* (elemental spiritual forces). Paul is not saying that paganism, Judaism, or a line-drawing version of Christianity are the same thing. Rather, he is saying that they can all be used by *stoicheia* as tools of enslavement.

PAUL	Formerly practiced Judaism	Enslaved by *stoicheia* (spiritual forces)
GALATIAN GENTILE CHRISTIANS	Formerly practiced paganism	Enslaved by *stoicheia* (spiritual forces)
GALATIAN GENTILE CHRISTIANS	As Christians adding Jewish boundary-line practices	Threat of enslavement again by *stoicheia* (spiritual forces)

What exactly are *stoicheia*? As commentators look at ways this word was used in earlier Greek writings they often mention the "ABC's." In Greek usage the letters of the alphabet were the *stoicheia* or irreducible constituents of words. *Stoicheia* refers to elements that make up a series, and the word took on a wide variety of specific meanings including the degrees on a sundial, notes for the musical scale, and the basic elements of the cosmos. "Philo speaks of the Greeks who revere the four elements (*stoicheia*)—earth, water, air, and fire—and give them the names of divinities" (Bruce 1982, 193). On this cosmic level the word ties in with religious practice of the time of viewing the heavenly elements as spiritual beings active in the physical world. Therefore, I affirm the NIV's translation "elemental spiritual forces," which captures the sense that *stoicheia* are spiritual (meaning they are more than human principles or powers), and they are forces (meaning they are more than just individual demons).

Colossians can help us further understand how Paul uses the term. In Colossians 2:8 he warns against captivity to the *stoicheia*. In Colossians 2:15 he proclaims that Jesus Christ has triumphed over the principalities and powers through the cross. He follows this by stating:

> [16] Therefore do not let anyone judge you by what you eat or drink, or with regard to a religious festival, a New Moon celebration or a Sabbath day. . . . [20] Since you died with Christ to the [*stoicheia*] elemental spiritual forces of this world, why, as though you still belonged to the world, do you submit to its rules: [21] "Do not handle! Do not taste! Do not touch!"? [22] These rules, which have to do with things that are all destined to perish with use, are based on merely human commands and teachings. [23] Such regulations indeed have an appearance of wisdom, with their self-imposed worship, their false humility and their harsh treatment of the body, but they lack any value in restraining sensual indulgence (Colossians 2:16, 20–23).

Similarly, Paul closely links these elemental spiritual forces and religious rules in Galatians 4:8-10. From Galatians and Colossians, we can observe that *stoicheia* enslave. While Paul connects them to religious rules and practices, he does not connect them to one specific religion. Paul does not distinguish good religions from bad religions. He does not equate elemental spiritual forces solely with paganism. In relation to concepts I have introduced in these first two chapters, we might say that the *stoicheia* take up the rules and rituals of paganism and turn them into bounded group religion. The *stoicheia* also take up the law, given by God, and turn it into bounded group religion. And in Antioch, we can observe how the *stoicheia* also take up the rules and practices of the followers of Jesus and turn them into bounded group religion. Note that it is not just an issue of good rules and bad rules, for God's law is good and Paul is not fully opposed to circumcision (6:15). Rather the problem is that elemental spiritual forces enslave us through turning rules and laws into ways of seeking status with God and humans and into judging and excluding others.

A simple turn of a phrase within this passage offers further evidence that religion is a fundamental part of the problem Paul addresses in this letter. He writes: "Now, however, that you have come to know God." But then it is as if he catches himself, thinking "no I don't want to say that. I do not want to offer them any grounds for giving importance to human actions in coming to know God." Therefore he adds, "or rather to be known by God" (4:9). This self-correction emphasizes God's action, the exact opposite of what religion focuses on.

The Colossians, Peter in Antioch, the other missionaries in Galatia, and the Gentile Christians in Galatia all experienced the saving work of Jesus through God's grace. Yet Paul confronts them all with words of warning about the enslaving power of religion in the hands of elemental spiritual forces. Therefore, rather than resting confidently in a "correct" understanding of salvation by grace, for instance, and assuming that Paul's words in Galatians do not apply to us, we would do well to regularly imagine Paul saying to us, "How is it that you are turning back to those weak and miserable forces [*stoicheia*]? Do you wish to be enslaved by them all over again?" (4:8-9).

The Problem in the Galatian Churches

As we work slowly through the whole letter we will grow in our understanding of the problem in Galatia. But ,based on the work we have done in these two chapters, let me offer an answer to our question about why Paul is so upset and what provoked him to write this letter. In short, he was deeply disturbed by the thought that the bounded group religiosity that caused the tragic church split he experienced in Antioch might do the same in the Galatian churches.

Before expanding that statement and describing the problem in more detail, it is important to re-state what was *not* the problem.

- His fundamental concern was not individuals in the Galatian churches struggling with a burden of guilt.

- The problem was not that the agitators explicitly taught that salvation is through human effort.

- Although in one sense circumcision and other Jewish practices were the central issue, they were not the funda-mental problem. Paul neither argues for a revised list of practices to use to draw the line of distinction between those who belong and those who do not, nor does he take the fuzzy approach and simply present erasing the line as a solution. He presents enslaving religion as a deeper problem and a centered approach rooted in Jesus' liberating work as the solution.

Paul was deeply disturbed by the bounded group religiosity of the agitators who used Jewish practices like circumcision to draw lines of distinction between those who belonged at the table of the people of God and those who did not. The other missionaries' actions and teachings threatened to undermine the work of God in the Galatian churches in a number of ways. Their actions, rooted in a distorted concept of honor, could miscommunicate that one ethnic group was superior to others and could cause the Gentile Christians to feel shamed and excluded. Paul perceived that the words and actions of the agitators could easily lead the Gentile Christians to once again submit to the enslaving power of religion. Under the influence of religion, the Galatian Christians could easily misinterpret the importance of human actions for salvation, acceptance by God, and one's position in the Christian community. Thus they too would begin to draw lines of division in a judgmental way as a basis for discerning who were true Christians who could sit at the Lord's Supper table together and those who were not worthy. As individuals they would no longer experience the richness of God's grace and freedom in Christ; as communities, unity based in Christ would be replaced by religious judgmentalism, ethnic discrimination, and division of the people of God. Paul writes this letter as an effort to stop this from happening.

Paul a Missionary Theologian

I began this book exploring the question of what picture Paul had in mind as he wrote the letter to the Galatians. Another important question to ask is, what picture of Paul do we have in mind as we read the letter? We know he was a church-planting missionary and that he was a profound theological thinker. The question is how those two relate in our minds when we read his letters.

One option is to imagine Paul, the letter writer, as first and foremost a scholarly theologian. Perhaps we picture him with some books or scrolls spread out on a desk and his thoughts taken up with articulating a coherent theological system. We might assume that besides writing letters he was working on a theological treatise with sections on different doctrines, or at least assume he had a full theology like that organized in his mind. This image of Paul leads readers to focus on questions like, what is his central theological theme? or, what is the organizing principle of this theology? It can lead to imagining Paul as being most concerned about correct communication of theological truths in an organized fashion.

A second option is to imagine Paul, first and foremost, as an itinerant church planting missionary. We picture him in a particular ministry setting but also imagine that he always has the struggles, conflicts, growth, and needs of other churches and leaders on his mind. Yes, he is a deep theological thinker, but he is not just head. He experiences the full range of human emotions as he deals with the challenges of his missionary work—joys, frustration, anger, confusion. Galatians itself supports this approach. As we will see, at numerous points in this letter he expresses strong emotions. Take a quick look at 4:12-16; these are not the dispassionate lines of a scholarly lecture but a missionary remembering moments of warmth in their relationship as well as feelings of sadness and concern in the present.

The theological questions Paul wrestles with arise not from leisurely reading and pondering but from real-life situations he encounters. In the case of Galatians, he is feeling deep concern over the potential split of the churches and the pain and confusion caused by the bounded approach of the agitators. His theological statements flow out of that concern. Similarly the theological responses he gives come not just from reading and reflecting on scripture, but are shaped also by experiences—God's action in his life and how he has seen God work in other settings.

I invite you to have the second picture in mind as you read Galatians and this book. The issue here is not about whether theology is important, or even the amount of theology in the letter. (I would argue that the second picture might actually help us see more theology in the letter.) It is not a question of whether Paul is a theologian or not, but what kind of theologian. That is why I use the term "missionary theologian." As a missionary, the situation and the issues provoke and lead Paul's theological thinking. He is responding to real life, grabbing for whatever variety of theological statements he thinks might be helpful to the Galatians in the midst of this crisis. We should expect the theology to be as complex and multilayered as the real-life situation, and we should not be surprised if in the passion and needs of the moment not all his ideas are necessarily consistent with something he has written elsewhere in another situation. Let us look for consistency in the God empowering and inspiring Paul as he writes this letter.

Having in mind what motivated Paul to write the letter, and using the content of these two chapters as aids in interpretation, we will begin, in the next chapter, to work our way through Paul's letter to the Galatians.

Personal Response

- What stands out to you from the description of the other missionaries? How do you think that might change your approach to reading this letter?

- Reflect on the commonalities you share with the other missionaries. Describe a situation in which you felt the pull to team up with others to create lines of distinction between insiders and outsiders?

- Describe a situation when others have made you feel on the "outside" of a boundary line.

- In what ways have you experienced or observed differences between a bounded church's theological statements and how these are lived out?

- What did you *think* and what did you *feel* as you read the definition and description of religion?

- What are ways these introductory chapters leave you confused or feeling apprehensive as we begin to study Galatians? What are ways these introductory chapters have contributed to a sense of excitement and anticipation as we begin to study Galatians?

CHAPTER THREE

No Other Gospel

The Text: Galatians 1:1-10

Paul, an apostle—sent not from men nor by a man, but by Jesus Christ and God the Father, who raised him from the dead— *²and all the brothers and sisters⁽ᵃ⁾ with me,*

To the churches in Galatia:

³ Grace and peace to you from God our Father and the Lord Jesus Christ, ⁴ who gave himself for our sins to rescue us from the present evil age, according to the will of our God and Father, ⁵ to whom be glory for ever and ever. Amen.

⁶ I am astonished that you are so quickly deserting the one who called you to live in the grace of Christ and are turning to a different gospel— ⁷ which is really no gospel at all. Evidently some people are throwing you into confusion and are trying to pervert the gospel of Christ. ⁸ But even if we or an angel from heaven should preach a gospel other than the one we preached to you, let them be under God's curse! ⁹ As we have already said, so now I say again: If anybody is preaching to you a gospel other than what you accepted, let them be under God's curse!

[10] *Am I now trying to win the approval of human beings, or of God? Or am I trying to please people? If I were still trying to please people, I would not be a servant of Christ.*

---

a. 1:2 The Greek word for *brothers and sisters* (*adelphoi*) refers here to believers, both men and women, as part of God's family; also in verse 11; and in 3:15; 4:12, 28, 31; 5:11, 13; 6:1, 18.

The Flow and Form of the Text

Each culture has norms and expectations for letter writing. I begin letters, even e-mails, differently when writing a Honduran friend than a friend in Canada or the United States. In the time of the Roman Empire the custom was to begin a letter with the name of the letter writer, something about his or her status or identity, then the name of the recipient, followed by words of greeting. Paul and other letter writers in the New Testament follow this custom. Knowing it is customary might lead us to quickly skim through the first lines to verse six where the letter "really" begins. That would be a mistake. There are significant differences here from the first lines of Paul's other letters. In these first lines he already emphasizes important themes in the letter and prepares the way for what follows.

One significant difference in this letter is the lack of positive words about the recipients. Generally after words of greetings Paul writes something like, "I thank my God every time I remember you. . ." (Philippians 1:3) and then offers words of affirmation. It appears that in dictating this letter Paul was so upset and felt such urgency that he jumped right to the issue with words of surprise, concern, accusation—and even a curse. Imagine the recipients of the letter, one of the churches gathered in the home they met in, listening to someone read the letter aloud. These direct and harsh words must have startled them, must have led them to ask, "Why is Paul so upset?"

The Text Explained

Words of greetings, filled with meaning (1:1-4). Paul does not identify himself in terms of his status in the Roman Empire, rather, as in most of his letters, as an apostle sent by God. Galatians is the only letter in which he adds the words, "sent not from men nor by a man" (1:1). In part this is to underscore his authority, and the authority of this letter. It is more than that, however. Right from the first line of the letter he contrasts human action and divine action. Repeatedly throughout the letter he will return to this theme. It is as if he keeps inviting the readers to imagine the two arrows I drew in chapter two, contrasting the way of religion and the way of God. After stating he was sent by Jesus Christ and God the Father, in this letter he also adds the phrase, "who raised him from the dead" (1:1). He thus affirms the singular importance of that action. Human actions such as circumcision and Jewish customs and practices pale in comparison.

Paul does not specifically name joint senders of the letter as he usually does, but he does make it clear he is not alone. He includes the phrase "and all the brothers and sisters with me" (1:2) and thus communicates that what he says in this letter has the support of others. It also underscores the community character of Paul's work and thought. The letter is not from an individual to other individuals about an individualistic gospel. Paul writes as part of a community to other communities—"the churches in Galatia" (1:2).

In his letters Paul always uses the salutation, "grace and peace" (1:3). These words, however, are much more than an automatic blessing empty of meaning. Grace is a major theme in this letter, thus we will explore the word in depth.

Significant Concept: Grace

Grace would not likely appear on most people's lists of complicated theological concepts. You may even wonder why it requires more than a sentence of explanation and thus be tempted to skip this section. Please read it! Digging deeper we will discover that not only was Paul's understanding of grace likely different than common explanations today, his conception of grace was also likely different than the other missionaries' understanding of grace. Grasping the difference in their thinking about grace is key to understanding their disagreement, and will lead to a more robust understanding of this beautiful word.

Grace is commonly defined as unmerited favor. It is a gift. In fact, the Greek word *charis* which is generally translated as "grace" in our Bibles is often translated as "gift" in other ancient works. One understanding of gift is something given with no strings attached—nothing was done to earn it and nothing is expected in return. That, however, is a relatively modern and Western understanding of gift. In many cultures in the world, gifts always carry an expectation of reciprocity. In those cultures, and in the world of Paul, gifts were seen as a means of beginning, deepening, or maintaining a relationship. If you receive a gift, you give a gift in return. Reciprocity is necessary for continuing the relationship. (And in reality, an element of reciprocity remains even in the modern West. Take a moment and think of times you have remembered that someone gave you a gift and therefore felt a sense of obligation to give a gift, or when the size of a gift you received influenced the size of the gift you gave to that person. We also practice non-tangible forms of reciprocity such as loyalty and friendship.) In Paul's time the word *charis* was used in the context of patron-client relations in which the patron gave something of value and a client, in return, gave service, honor, or something of lesser value to the patron. Gifts differed from loans or a transaction in that a response could not be demanded, but reciprocity was nevertheless assumed. The point here is not to imply that people in the time of Paul did not really have a concept of "true" grace, but rather that their concept of true grace was different than what many in the West today understand as grace. What was true grace for them? What made something a gift?

John Barclay explores these questions in his books, *Paul and the Gift* and *Paul and the Power of Grace*. Through careful study of many texts of the time, both Jewish and from the broader society, he found a number of different characteristics that would categorize something as a gift, or an action as gracious grace. A particular author's concept of grace might focus on just one of these or include a combination of a few of them.

Superabundance – the size or duration; its being huge, lavish, or long-lasting makes it grace.

Singularity – something is considered grace because the giver's attitude is solely focused on acting in ways that benefit others.

Priority – something is considered a gift because it is given before any initiative of the recipient. In this view it is grace not because there is no response expected, but because the gift is given first.

Incongruity – a gift is given without regard to the status of the recipient. The recipient is not worthy of receiving a gift from the giver. This was uncommon in the ancient world. In their honor-oriented society people gave gifts discriminately, considering their status and the status of the recipient. They only gave to people deemed worthy to receive the gift.

In all four of these there is an expectation that the recipient will give something in response.

Non-circularity – grace means there is no expectation of response. There is no cycle of reciprocity. This view, close to the "no strings attached" concept, was very uncommon in the ancient world (Barclay 2015, 70–74; 2020, 13–16).

Paul emphatically and repeatedly proclaimed a gospel of grace. Paul also clearly disagreed with the agitators' articulation of the gospel. Therefore, as described in the second chapter, many have assumed that the other missionaries taught salvation by works. Barclay, however, invites us to imagine another option. Rather than assuming that what is at the root of the disagreement is speaking of grace or not speaking of grace, he suggests we see the disagreement in their understanding of grace. To aid us in conceiving of the problem in that way, Barclay explores a number of texts from Paul's Second Temple era (Wisdom of Solomon, Philo, Psuedo-Philo [LAB], Qumran Hodayot, and 4 Ezra) (2015, 310-320; 2020, 28-36). Two things are noteworthy: each document spoke of God's grace, and each used different combinations of the characteristics listed above in their descriptions of grace.

Although priority and superabundance were commonly used, no one characteristic of grace was found in all the documents. None of the authors wrote of God's grace in terms of non-circularity; their understanding of gift included an expectation of a response by the receiver. Some texts portrayed grace as incongruous, but more commonly communicated an understanding of discernment and selectivity in the giving—God acting graciously to those who were worthy. For instance, Barclay describes Philo as emphasizing God's grace preceding any action to earn what was received (priority), and also communicating a sense of worthiness of those who received it (congruity). Philo makes clear that the recipient's worthiness was a condition of the gift, but not the cause of the gift; it was not given in response to their worthiness. But he also communicated a sense that the unworthy would not receive the gift because it would not be proper for God to give to those unfit to be honored in this way. It appears the other missionaries in Galatia held a similar view of grace—people who did not identify with the people of God by following certain Jewish practices were unworthy of God's grace.

We can affirm that both Paul and the agitators proclaimed God's gracious action, yet also recognize from Paul's strong language in this section of chapter one that he had a very different concept of the characteristics of grace. Like the other missionaries, Paul affirmed that God as gift-giver takes the initiative, but unlike the agitators Paul understood God's gift as given regardless of people's status or worth. As Barclay states:

> Paul's theology of grace was a radical intervention into a culture of honor-acquisition and status-competition. Paul's gospel announces that God's definitive gift in Christ does not, as one might expect, follow pre-constituted standards of worth, but is given without regard to worth and grants the only worth that truly counts. Paul's contemporaries, both Jewish and non-Jewish, were inclined to take for granted that God's benevolence, though lavish, was given discriminately, as all good gifts

were given to those considered worthy of them by one criterion or another (ethnicity, social status, gender, education, morality, or age). It was common to imagine that God's generosity (and the generosity of the righteous) would be limited to those who were qualified, in one way or another, for his gifts. But Paul announces the divine gift given without regard to worth (his definition of grace), and he thus creates the possibility of new configurations of society and new understandings of value (Barclay 2016, 1).

How then does this inform our understanding of the tension between Paul and the agitators? The contrast is not between one side, Paul, preaching grace, and the other side preaching salvation by works. Rather it is between two differing concepts of grace. In contrast to Paul the other missionaries thought only certain groups of people were worthy of God's grace. In terms of this commentary we could say that the other missionaries' concept of grace could coexist with, or even facilitate, a church functioning as a bounded group—the gift is for the worthy ones on the right side of the lines. In contrast, Paul's concept of grace is a gift of God that erases lines of distinction and facilitates a centered approach.

Returning to where we started, let us observe how Paul's concept of grace is similar to and different from the contemporary Western view of grace.

	MODERN WESTERN CONCEPT OF GOD'S GRACE	PAUL'S CONCEPT OF GOD'S GRACE
Individual does not have to be worthy, does not earn what is received	YES	YES
Communal character of unworthiness	NO	YES
A response to religious group self-righteousness, class hierarchy, and ethnic discrimination	NO	YES
Reciprocity by receiver expected	NO	YES

The modern Western concept and Paul's concept of grace agree on the first point. Both understand grace as God's initiative that an individual does not earn or merit in any way. They differ on both the second, third, and fourth points. In Paul's honor-shame culture worthiness is determined not just by the individual's actions or status, but also the worthiness of the group to which a person belongs. And grace is not just liberation from an internal sense of guilt, but also liberates from the shame imposed by those who label a person as unworthy. To the Western individual view, Paul would say, "Yes, that and so much more."

The two views also differ in their understanding of recipients' responses to grace. In the modern West, many Christians resist making any connections between God's grace and expectations of reciprocity by the receiver. The assumption is that to talk of how recipients of grace are expected to respond to the gift by changing behavior or joining together to worship implies it was not actually a gift. As stated above, this is a relatively new understanding of gift, from the last few centuries, and not held in all the world today. As is evident in the last two chapters of Galatians, for Paul and his contemporaries an expectation of response by recipients was an accepted and expected part of gift giving. Indeed, as Ryan Schellenberg observes, "A key purpose of gift giving was to forge transformative relationships of generosity, gratitude, loyalty and trust."*

As we work our way through the letter we will deepen our understanding of God's grace, how Paul came to this understanding of it, and its implications. In the last chapters of the book we will explore what Paul envisioned as reciprocating responses to God's grace.

—

With this understanding of Paul's concept of grace, we can imagine that as Paul dictated these words of salutation he said them with deep conviction, praying they might experience anew and live in the reality of this gift from God. Likewise, the word "peace" has special significance in this situation. The Greek word translated "peace" meant an absence of violence. Paul likely had the Hebrew word *"shalom"* in mind, which has a much broader meaning, including wellbeing, harmony in relations, completeness, health. Because of not living in the full reality of the gracious action of God, the Galatian churches are not experiencing *shalom*, but conflict and division.

---

* Comment to author, 8/6/2021.

Only in his letter to the Galatians does Paul expand the "grace and peace" greeting to a concise narrative summary of the gospel he proclaims. "Jesus Christ, who gave himself for our sins to rescue us from the present evil age, according to the will of our God and Father" (1:3-4). This summary includes not only a sense of freedom from the consequences of our sins, but also freedom from the present evil age. Paul describes God as Father, and by using "our," includes the Galatians as God's children. This reaffirms the relational heart of the Christian faith; it is not a matter of rules and religion. And it anticipates what Paul will proclaim in Galatians 4:4-7. The Galatians already are children of God. They do not have to be circumcised in order to be part of the family.

Through this short greeting (1:1-4) Paul has made clear that God's action is central. He does not mention any human actions; three times it is God who acts (to make Paul an apostle, to raise Jesus from the dead, and to free us from the present evil age.) The rescue is not conditional. Paul does not say that Jesus provides freedom for those who have certain status, belong to a specific ethnic group, do certain things, or obey specific rules. This emphasis on God's action contrasts with the emphasis on human action in what, in this commentary, I am calling religion.

As we go through the letter we will continue to develop the theme of what Paul means by "present evil age" and how that contrasts with the new creation he mentions at the end of the letter (6:15). One way we can further comprehend its meaning is to think of it as the opposite of grace and *shalom*. In the present evil age, law reigns, not grace. A variety of laws and standards measure people's status and worth: religious law, economic law, the law of merit, honor codes, and social, gender, and ethnic categories. In terms of this commentary we would include bounded group religiosity. As we saw in the previous chapter, however, Paul would urge us to not just think about particular rules as problematic, but the power (*stoichea*) that takes up laws, standards, and lines of a bounded group and uses them as a tool of enslavement. The word "rescue" relates to liberation and freedom, a repeated theme in the letter. Here and throughout the letter we do well to press beyond the surface and think of enslaving powers.

Distortion of the gospel provokes a strong response (1:6-10). Right now I feel the need for words of transition, but there is no transition in the letter. From words of praise for God's liberating action Paul abruptly writes, "I am astonished!" We have already stated it in the previous chapter, but it merits repeating. This is a passionate letter! Paul is upset. Let us enter into his passion and not just treat the themes of this letter in an intellectual way.

Note that in verse six he writes of a present, and ongoing, "deserting," not a past tense "deserted." This helps us understand Paul's sense of urgency. This is a dynamic situation; the Galatians are turning to a different gospel, being pulled in that direction by the agitators. Paul writes the letter to stop this turning away and re-center them on the gospel of Jesus Christ.

Paul has already mentioned grace in the greeting and it is noteworthy that in the very first line of the body of the letter he speaks of living in the grace of Christ. In light of what is written above about Paul's understanding of grace, take a moment and ponder what he meant by this phrase. To live in the grace of Christ is to commune together as a group of people freed from bounded group practices of including some and not others based on earthly measures of worth. To return to the line-drawing practices of the world is to abandon the gospel. His beginning with this phrase, "living in the grace of Christ," affirms what we observed in the previous two chapters about his central concern as he writes the letter.

The Greek word we translate as "gospel" means good news. For us, "gospel" is almost exclusively a Christian word. In Paul's time, however, it was commonly used to announce military victories (the gospel of Caesar's victory) and used to proclaim the glories of and give honor to the emperor in the imperial cult. (The imperial cult, which worshiped the emperor as divine, was practiced alongside other religions. For instance, one could be devoted to Phrygian cult of worship of the mother of the gods and also participate in the imperial cult.) It is possible that Christians began to use the term "gospel" to underscore their confession that Jesus, not Caesar, was Lord. Surely Paul, and other Christians, were influenced by the use of the Hebrew form of the word in Isaiah 52:7 and 61:1 (see Romans 10:15). With both the Roman and Hebrew use of the word, Richard Hays writes,

> We should understand that the gospel is the triumphantly proclaimed message that God has at last taken control and begun to reign. That helps to explain why Paul regards the Missionaries' message as a non-gospel; in his view, it merely extends the status quo that pertained under the Law prior to the coming of Jesus. Their "gospel" does not reflect the world-transforming effect of his death and resurrection (Hays 2000, 205).

Paul probably uses the term "other gospel" because the other missionaries referred to what they preached as the gospel. In verse 7, however, Paul immediately makes clear there is no other gospel. There is only one gospel and the agitators are twisting and perverting it.

To briefly review what we observed in chapter two, the teaching of the other missionaries included an emphasis on the necessity of circumcision (5:3; 6:13, 15) and following at least some aspects of the law of Moses and other Jewish practices and celebrations that distinguished Jews from Gentiles (2:16; 3:2; 5:3-4; 4:10, 21). They proclaimed the graciousness of God in providing salvation through Jesus Christ, but unlike Paul they viewed grace as limited to those who are worthy recipients—Israel the chosen people of God, or those who became worthy through living like Jews.

For Paul, what the agitators were doing was so problematic he pronounced a curse, twice, against any who preached a gospel different from what he had proclaimed (1:8-9). To repeat, Paul is clearly very upset. It is easy to imagine at this point the Galatian recipients thinking, "Isn't Paul overreacting a bit? It is not like these preachers who have come have tried to get us to deny Jesus and go worship pagan divinities or participate in rituals with prostitutes at pagan temples." Like Paul they preached that salvation was through the cross and resurrection of Jesus. They just added some things to complement or improve what Paul had preached. Paul preached Jesus. The agitators preached "Jesus and . . .": Jesus *and* circumcision, Jesus *and* the Law, Jesus *and* Jewish traditions. As we observed in chapter one, this could easily communicate that the other missionaries considered the Galatian Christians not fully converted. But, in light of what we have learned about differing understandings of grace, it would be more accurate to say they viewed the Galatians as not fully worthy of grace. The *and* is the big problem that changes everything. Paul preached Jesus, period. He did not add other things people needed to do to become worthy. While he certainly believed there were proper, reciprocal *responses* to the gift of grace, Paul did not believe there were preconditions required to *receive* the gift of grace. God's grace is available to all. The saving action of God through Jesus is not limited to certain worthy groups. All can be saved, included in the family of God, and liberated from the powers of the present evil age. By preaching "Jesus *and*" the message changes from a radical gospel of freedom for all regardless of status to a message that draws a line between the worthy and the unworthy.

In the previous chapters I emphasized that the other missionaries did not explicitly teach that salvation is through human effort. They stated that salvation was a gift of God, that we are saved by grace. In terms of the arrows in the previous chapter we might say they did not explicitly teach the perspective of the religious arrow—that humans actions determine how God will respond to humans. Yet Paul responds as if the problem in Galatia is bounded group religiosity. It will aid us in reflecting about this text in our own context if we imagine some ways that their not-fully-worthy attitude toward the Gentiles and their "Jesus *and*" message led to the problem of works righteousness and enslaving religiosity Paul is responding to. We start with two observations, not about the agitators, but humans and religion as a power (a spiritual force). Humans have a natural religious inclination, so the human tendency is to interpret things in a religious way. Second, the power religion† (*stoicheia*) actively uses something like the other missionaries' additions to the gospel and turns them into bounded group religiosity. (See pages 45-49 for an explanation of religion as a spiritual power, one within the Pauline category of principalities and powers.) How might what the agitators said and did lend itself to these religious perversions of the gospel?

---

† I use this phrase, "the power religion," to refer to religion as an enslaving power, one example of what Paul refers to as principalities and powers. I am not referring to the power of religion, but to religion as a power.

- Because of their understanding of grace, different from Paul's, they may have stated that to be worthy of God's grace one must live like a Jew. The Galatians could easily interpret that in a religious way.

- Even if the other missionaries did not state explicitly that the Gentile Christians were inferior, just as we observed in the visitors from Antioch in the first chapter of this book, the Jewish-Christian missionaries' actions and attitudes of ethno-religious superiority may have led the Galatians to feel inferior, on the wrong side of a religious line.

- Perhaps the other missionaries used phrases like "to fully experience the blessings of being a child of God" or "to be a true member of the people of God" or "to be a true Christian." Even if not meant to communicate a religious sense of salvation by works, they could be heard that way.

- Perhaps it was a question of quantity. By the other missionaries talking more about human actions (rules, standards, and practices) than God's action, the former may have overwhelmed the latter in the minds of the Galatians.

Paul ends this section of the letter (1:10) with questions and a reflection that serve as transition and connection to the next section. Apparently the agitators had accused Paul of seeking favor with the Galatians by preaching only a part of the gospel and not insisting on obedience to the law and on circumcision. We can tell from the tone and confrontational words in this letter that Paul was not focused on pleasing people. But he lets us know this has not always been the case. He writes, "If I were still trying to please people, I would not be a servant of Christ" (1:10).

I invite you to turn back to the end of the previous chapter and read the last paragraph in the section near the end, "The Problem in the Galatian Churches." As you read it think about what you might add to that paragraph now, or how what we have seen in Galatians 1:1-10 enriches our understanding of that paragraph.

As I re-read that paragraph through the lens of this chapter, what impresses me is the theological factors we can now add. What the last chapter described are problems that flow from misconstruing who God is and what God has done. Paul is upset because the agitators' impoverished view of God's grace and their line-drawing ways ignore the reality that God through Christ has liberated Christians from the present evil age. The religiosity of a bounded church is part of the present evil age. Differentiating people as worthy and unworthy is part of the present evil age. The God, or gods, of religion is part of the present evil age. Paul is upset because the other missionaries' you-must-be-worthy gospel perverts not only people's understanding of the gospel, but also their experience of it. It leads to the problems described at the end of the last chapter. Paul is upset because the Galatian Christians are returning to an enslavement from which they have already been freed (1:4, 4:8-9).

Our deeper understanding of grace and Paul's energetic confrontation of the agitators reinforces and expands what we pointed to in the first chapter of this book. Paul's concern is much broader than just a mistaken point of doctrine. As John Barclay observes, "Paul resists attempts to impose on believers preconstituted systems of worth, whether ethnic, social, or moral. Paul remaps a reality in the wake of the unconditioned gift of God in Christ and builds experimental, trans-ethnic communities that take their bearings from this singular event" (Barclay 2020, 40–41).

Implications of the Text for Today

Correct doctrinal statements alone are not enough. They did not prevent the other missionaries from twisting the gospel in ways that led to religious enslavement. We do well to frequently reflect on how we may be succumbing to acting like the other missionaries. The reality that a church affirms that salvation is by grace, not works, does not necessarily mean there is not distortion of the gospel. Many speak of salvation but through their actions and attitudes live out bounded group religiosity. Similar to what I imagine happened with these missionaries, many today communicate that to be a true Christian one must comply with certain rules, meet certain standards, and participate faithfully in church activities. It is easy to imagine that both insiders and outsiders experience a bounded church as proclaiming a you-must-be-worthy gospel.

Perhaps when you read those lines, like me, what first came to mind was legalistic churches. True, legalistic churches are bounded. My life experience, however, points to the reality that boundedness is not limited to legalism. In the beginning of my book, *Centered-Set Church: Discipleship and Community Without Judgmentalism*, I describe the legalism of my youth and then recount how I rejected it. Yet, although I may have left legalism behind, I did not leave line-drawing behind. Instead of using rules about drinking and dancing, I used other things to draw lines to separate true Christians from mediocre Christians or to separate Christians from non-Christians, such as: a recognition of Jesus as Lord not just Savior, openness to gifts of the Spirit, a commitment to social justice and helping the poor, and, ironically, I self-righteously drew a line between myself and legalistic Christians. After a number of years, through the excellent observations and penetrating questions of some older and wiser Christians, I came to see that I was just as religious as ever and as enslaved to bounded group religiosity as I had been in my youth. An implication of this section is to recognize the importance of reflecting honestly on our religious and line-drawing tendencies in order to become freer from them.

The depth and radicalness of God's grace. The previous section had a negative warning, correct statements are not enough. Positively, this section of Galatians calls us to recognize how the work of God is more radical than some of our doctrinal statements. Yes, grace is unmerited favor, but it is so much more. As John Barclay writes,

Both Paul and Jesus stood alongside people who were not at all respectable. In doing so, they took big social risks. God's grace operates beyond our norms of what is civil, proper or fair. And it challenges our hidden prejudices. Why do we distrust immigrants and stigmatize the poor, or disdain certain socioeconomic groups? Why are we tempted to think that people who do not have a spouse or a job, or who do not have a physique matching cultural ideals, have somehow failed? Whose values are we applying? (Barclay and Hill 2016).

We are called to live in God's grace (1:6). That includes a radical message of our inclusion. Reflect on the examples Barclay lists on page 71 and reflect back on my comments on bounded line-drawing in the previous section. In the face of any shame, rejection, discrimination, or exclusion you have experienced, Paul proclaims to you that God does not draw lines as others do. Live in the reality that God loves you and accepts you regardless of others' definitions of your status and worth.

We are called to live in God's grace (1:6). That includes a radical challenge to turn away from the line-drawing judgmentalism, shaming, racism, and prejudices of our cultures and society. The agitators lived out a religious and ethnic sense of supremacy that shamed and excluded others. That is not the way of Jesus. Paul boldly challenged them. Having experienced the radical inclusiveness of God's grace, let us welcome and include people regardless of how others measure their status and worth.

Proclaim the gospel, again, and again. Let us not miss one of the most obvious implications of this section, and the letter as a whole. Evangelizing is not just a one-time activity aimed at non-believers. Paul writes this letter to people who have converted, have experienced God's grace, yet he proclaims the gospel anew. Because of our natural religious tendencies, because our society is saturated with the law of merit, because we so often find ourselves on the wrong side of us-them lines, or view others on the wrong side of lines we draw, we need to regularly be re-evangelized, to hear clear statements of God's radical and unconditional love, to be reoriented to the ways of God's grace.

Confront religious distortions of the gospel. Jesus was radical in his confrontation of bounded group religiosity, so radical that defenders of the religious status quo conspired to kill him. Paul displays more passion about the problems in Galatia than in his other letters. Paul was very upset. Do we feel as passionate and concerned to confront bounded group religiosity as Paul was? At times we need to join Paul and say, "No, this is not the gospel." The challenge is to confront in a centered rather than a bounded way.

We will learn how to go about this by following Paul's example throughout this letter. In these verses we observe two important elements of confronting religiosity in a centered way. First, Paul made very clear he was not confronting one bounded group's line with another line. The problem was not what came after the "and" in the "Jesus *and* . . ." gospel. It was the "*and.*" It was the attitude wedded to that "and" of the Gentile Christians not being fully worthy. Second, Paul's "no" against the distorted gospel of the agitators was based in a "yes"—a yes of God's gracious love. Part of the rescue from the present evil age, by the cross of Jesus, is identifying the enslaving forces of this world. The "no" of Paul in this section is part of the positive proclamation of freedom in this letter. Part of the "yes" of freedom is saying "no" to bounded group religiosity that excludes outsiders and enslaves insiders.

Recognize other enslaving forces. The primary focus of this book will be on the enslaving power of bounded group religiosity. Yet the "present evil age" includes many other enslaving forces. Ethnic superiority, or racism, is one I have mentioned. One implication of this section of Galatians is an invitation to reflect on other enslaving forces that we can be freed from through Jesus. For instance the spirit of consumerism today tells us that the more money and possessions we have the better our life will be. It is an enslaving lie. Consumerism also contributes to measuring people's status and worth based on their wealth. Through Christ we can, and must, say a "no" to the lies of consumerism and say "yes" to the reality that our identity is in Jesus Christ. We might add nationalism, or Mammon. What are other enslaving forces today?

Personal Response

- Where have you observed religious tendencies in your life to live as if God's love is conditional?

- I invite you to reflect on ways you have felt excluded, shamed, discriminated against, looked down upon, or rejected—by churches and in society. In response to each recollection, imagine God proclaiming, "I love and accept you." Imagine Paul offering you a seat at a dinner table, in the name of Jesus, with people from various categories and of varying status.

- Where have you seen bounded group line-drawing tendencies in your life? In your church?

- Do you sense a need to more frequently be reminded of God's gracious, anti-religious gospel? If so, how might you hear or read it more often?

- Do you sense a call to more frequently tell others, Christians and non-Christians, of God's gracious, anti-religious gospel? If so, how might you do so?

- What might be the significance for your life, individually and as a church, to embrace Paul's understanding of grace as explained in this chapter?

- What other enslaving forces have you experienced in the present evil age? How might the church more actively enable people to live in freedom from them? Do you feel a call to take a step of freedom today?

CHAPTER FOUR

Different Fruit: Stories of Human Action and God's Action

The Text: Galatians 1:11-2:10

[11] *I want you to know, brothers and sisters, that the gospel I preached is not of human origin.* [12] *I did not receive it from any man, nor was I taught it; rather, I received it by revelation from Jesus Christ.*

[13] *For you have heard of my previous way of life in Judaism, how intensely I persecuted the church of God and tried to destroy it.* [14] *I was advancing in Judaism beyond many of my own age among my people and was extremely zealous for the traditions of my fathers.* [15] *But when God, who set me apart from my mother's womb and called me by his grace, was pleased* [16] *to reveal his Son in me so that I might preach him among the Gentiles, my immediate response was not to consult any human being.* [17] *I did not go up to Jerusalem to see those who were apostles before I was, but I went into Arabia. Later I returned to Damascus.*

¹⁸ Then after three years, I went up to Jerusalem to get acquainted with Cephas[a] and stayed with him fifteen days. ¹⁹ I saw none of the other apostles—only James, the Lord's brother. ²⁰ I assure you before God that what I am writing you is no lie.

²¹ Then I went to Syria and Cilicia. ²² I was personally unknown to the churches of Judea that are in Christ. ²³ They only heard the report: "The man who formerly persecuted us is now preaching the faith he once tried to destroy." ²⁴ And they praised God because of me.

2 Then after fourteen years, I went up again to Jerusalem, this time with Barnabas. I took Titus along also. ² I went in response to a revelation and, meeting privately with those esteemed as leaders, I presented to them the gospel that I preach among the Gentiles. I wanted to be sure I was not running and had not been running my race in vain. ³ Yet not even Titus, who was with me, was compelled to be circumcised, even though he was a Greek. ⁴ This matter arose because some false believers had infiltrated our ranks to spy on the freedom we have in Christ Jesus and to make us slaves. ⁵ We did not give in to them for a moment, so that the truth of the gospel might be preserved for you.

⁶ As for those who were held in high esteem—whatever they were makes no difference to me; God does not show favoritism—they added nothing to my message. ⁷ On the contrary, they recognized that I had been entrusted with the task of preaching the gospel to the uncircumcised,[b] just as Peter had been to the circumcised.[c] ⁸ For God, who was at work in Peter as an apostle to the circumcised, was also at work in me as an apostle to the Gentiles. ⁹ James, Cephas[d] and John, those esteemed as pillars, gave me and Barnabas the right hand of fellowship when they recognized the grace given to me. They agreed that we should go to the Gentiles, and they to the circumcised. ¹⁰ All they asked was that we should continue to remember the poor, the very thing I had been eager to do all along.

---

a. 1:18 That is, Peter
b. 2:7 That is, Gentiles
c. 2:7 That is, Jews; also in verses 8 and 9
d. 2:9 That is, Peter; also in verses 11 and 14

The Flow and Form of the Text

In this section of the letter Paul uses narrative form. He begins autobiographically, and then he widens the lens beyond his personal story to recount events in Jerusalem that involved many others. Yet, the history he relates remains autobiographical. He participated in the events and gives the report in first person. This narrative section of the letter continues into the next part of Galatians 2 which we will explore it in the following chapter.

Many think of Paul as the theologian of the New Testament and approach his writings as if he was writing theological treatises. As I stated in chapter two, Paul's writings are theologically rich, but we do well to remember he was first and foremost a missionary, a church planter, a pastor. His theology is done in the context of mission. The theological points he makes in the letter are for the purpose of addressing the situation in Galatia. He is not writing an essay on the doctrine of salvation organized in outline form and removed from a particular context. At this point in the letter he switches to narrative for the purpose of making connections with the situation in Galatia, to aid in the understanding of those who will listen to the letter, and to be more persuasive.

To say he is not writing an abstract theological essay does not, however, mean there is not theological content. In this section Paul communicates significant theological information through narrative. Rather than trying to force Paul into our framework of what systematic theology should look like, perhaps we would do well to follow his lead of communicating theology through various genres, including narrative.

The Text Explained

Radical life change through God's gracious action (1:11-24).
Commentators commonly state that Paul's purpose in verses 11
and 12 specifically, and the rest of chapter one more generally, is to
buttress his authority. The other missionaries likely did question
Paul's authority and these verses certainly defend it. Yet we see
much more than that if we keep in mind what we have learned
about the problem in Galatia and the introductory material about
religion and bounded churches.

In terms of the arrows diagram in chapter one, in verse 11
Paul affirms that what he preaches is not a religious tradition
constructed by humans to get something from God, rather it came
down to him from God (1:12). The end of verse 12 can be translated
either as "revelation from Jesus Christ" or "revelation of Jesus
Christ." Keeping both in mind has the advantage of emphasizing
that the gospel is not just information, but an encounter. The
content of the gospel he preached cannot be separated from his
encounter with Jesus—the revelation of Jesus Christ to him. As
Paul has already proclaimed (1:4) he emphasizes anew that what
is needed is not a set of human practices and human beliefs—that
is, religion—but the radical action of God. The gospel and the
Christian life are radically different than religion. Religion comes
naturally to us, but the Christian life requires an act of God in us.

The first word of verse 13 "for"—connects what follows with
the preceding two verses. Paul fills out the previous statement
with narrative details. The people in the Galatian churches already
know about his past. Therefore, the purpose of these verses is to
remind them of certain aspects of his past that are relevant to
what the agitators have been saying and doing in Galatia. Paul first
mentions his previous life in Judaism, including active persecution
of the Church (1:13).

Today we commonly use the word "Judaism" as synonymous with the religion of the Jews, but it appears Paul, and others at his time, used the word more narrowly. One hint of this is that this is the only place in the New Testament we encounter this Greek word that is translated as "Judaism" (1:13 & 14). We do not find the term in the Old Testament, but it is in Maccabees, texts written two centuries before Galatians. The writers of those texts expressed concern that foreign cultures, like Hellenism, were influencing Jews. The writers of Maccabees used the term "Judaism" not to refer to Jewish tradition in a general way, but to a set of beliefs and practices that marked off Jews, and Jewish culture, as distinct from Gentiles (2 Maccabees 2:21; 8:1; 4 Maccabees 4:26). Judaism, however, was more than just the practices themselves. As Matthew Novenson observes, when ancient writers in both the Hellenistic and Roman period referred to Jewish religion and culture they used terms like, "laws," "customs," and "traditions." They rarely used the term "Judaism," but when they did "they meant not the ancestral customs themselves but a sectarian program for the defense and promotion of those customs" (Novenson 2014, 35–36).

For Paul, being a Jew and Judaism are two different things. He still considered himself a Jew (2:15, Romans 11:1). And although an encounter with Jesus Christ led Paul to turn away from Judaism, that does not mean that by Judaism he refers to all non-Christian Jews. Judaism refers to what Paul describes in these verses., namely a movement to guard Jewish life from corrupting outside influences. Those in the movement did so through aggressively promoting and defending Jewish practices. It was clearly a bounded group.

It is not an easy thing, for me as writer or you as reader, to use a word differently than its common definition. In the case of "Judaism," I think it is worth our effort. First, it further reinforces the point that although Paul does not use the term "bounded group," he has in mind what I have described as a bounded group. Second, if we think of Judaism as all of the non-Christian Jews at that time it can lead us to seeing Jewish beliefs and practices as the problem. If I do that I can easily think of this being about other people, not me. Seeing that Paul is referring to a bounded group movement of some Jews, we must recognize that we can fall into the same problem. We too have the potential to worship the right God in the wrong way. Third, it helps protect us from the mistake Christians have too frequently made over the centuries of being antisemitic because of verses like these.

I am not arguing we should change the way we commonly use the word "Judaism." But in this commentary, in the few places I will use the word, I will be using it as Paul does here to refer to a particular group of Jewish people with bounded group ways who were driven by sincere concerns over outside influences but zealously imposed their perspectives on others.

The spirit of bounded group religiosity drives people to passionately maintain the lines and condemn, persecute, even kill those who transgress or challenge the lines. Paul will refer to the divisive and destructive fruit of religion numerous times in the letter. He begins here with a personal example. His commitment to his religion and his efforts to achieve honor within his bounded group propelled him to violently persecute followers of Jesus. The damage produced was not, however, limited just to the division between Judaism and the Church. It impacted insiders as well. Paul's use of the word "advancing" points to the sense of competition often found within bounded groups. People judge some as having more status than others. People of that time viewed honor as a limited good. If one gains honor, someone else loses it. To advance was to put others down. The competition and violence of bounded group religiosity that Paul describes were part of the "present evil age" (1:4).

Through these brief narrative comments (1:13-14) Paul communicates clearly to the Galatians that he knows well what the other missionaries are advocating. And, it is significant that he is not just saying, "Yes, I have been involved in what they are talking about." He was fully committed. His words imply that he followed the traditions of the Jews with more zeal and success than the agitators themselves. This enables him to say with greater credibility, "This is not the way."

These same words have additional import for modern interpreters influenced, as described in the first chapter, by Luther's experience. Note how Paul's narrative contrasts with Luther's experience. Paul says nothing about striving but not finding escape from his burden of guilt until meeting Jesus. Paul's sense of guilt for his conduct came after meeting Jesus. This calls for reflection. If not saved from a feeling of guilt what was Paul saved from?

Through the "but" at the beginning of verse 15, Paul lets us know that a contrast is coming. A key aspect of the contrast is a change in emphasis from human action to God's action. In the previous two verses Paul is the one who acts: "my way of life," "I persecuted," "[I] tried to destroy," "I was advancing," "[I] was extremely zealous." Now God is the one who acts: "God . . . set me apart," "[God] called me," "[God] was pleased to reveal." When Paul does mention human action (his preaching) he makes clear it is a response to God's action. Religion operates under the opposite logic.

The way of religion: Humans act seeking to move God to act.

Humans act. → God responds.

The way of the God of the Bible revealed by Jesus Christ is grace: God acts and humans respond.

> God acts graciously. → Humans respond.

Of course, as I have stated earlier, the other missionaries in Galatia affirmed, like Paul, that God as gift-giver takes the initiative, but as we observed in chapter three their understanding of God's grace was not as radical as Paul's. In fact the agitators' understanding of grace requires another step in the diagram.

God evaluates the worthiness of humans.

> If worthy, God acts graciously. → Humans respond.
>
> If not worthy, God does not act. X

In these verses (13-16) Paul makes explicitly clear that he was *not* worthy. He was persecuting the church of Jesus Christ. As Barclay observes, "What has reconstituted Paul's life is a divine act of grace without regard to his ethnicity, tradition, and excellence, and without regard to his former opposition to God" (Barclay 2015, 359). (". . .while we were God's enemies" [Romans 5:10].)

> Paul is unworthy, an opponent of Jesus Christ.
> Even so God acts graciously toward Paul. God does not reject
> or punish him; God calls Paul. → Paul responds.

Let us think about these verses through the lens of what Paul wrote at the beginning of the letter. "Grace and peace to you from God our Father and Lord Jesus Christ, who gave himself for our sins to rescue us from the present evil age" (1:3-4). Rather than rejecting or punishing Paul God rescued him from the bounded group religiosity of the present evil age and graciously brought him into a new reality, a new creation (6:15). Paul did not get there by his own logic, this was an act of God. In fact his logic had led him to the opposite. It required an encounter with God.

Paul states forcefully that he was not schooled by other humans, specifically other apostles (1:16-19). As we previously observed, in addition to the theological point of emphasizing God's action, this likely is a move to bolster his authority—what he preaches he received direct from God. He also reinforces his authority by borrowing language and images from Jeremiah and Isaiah: "set me apart from my mother's womb and called me" and "preach him among the Gentiles" (see Jeremiah 1:4-5; Isaiah 49:1, 5-6, note that what is translated as "nations" in our English Bibles is the word "*ethne*" or "Gentiles" in the Greek translation of the Old Testament, the Septuagint). Through this he communicates three significant things. By implication he puts himself in the same category of these important prophets. And, as he will do in other places in the letter, he accentuates that his mission and message is firmly rooted in the God of Israel. And, subtly, he points out that the inclusion of Gentiles is not a new idea he came up with.

Although I have emphasized the discontinuity between Paul's current life and mission and his previous life in Judaism, I want to underscore his continuity with the God of Israel, the Hebrew Scriptures, and the prophets. When Paul critiques Judaism he is not practicing what today we would call anti-Semitism. He critiqued a religious perversion of the covenant between God and Israel. Paul today would similarly critique religious perversions of the Christian faith. As we observed in Galatians 4, and discussed in chapter two of this book, for Paul the problem of bounded group religiosity is not limited to one group or ethnicity.

Paul ends this part of the narrative by mentioning the affirm-ation of the churches of Judea (1:23-24). It is a concrete example of new creation in contrast to the present evil age. Religion had produced violence and division. God's action produced reconciliation. Those who had feared Paul now praise God because of him. Before there was persecution, now there is preaching.

Truth of the gospel of grace that includes uncircumcised Gentiles affirmed by Jerusalem leaders (2:1-10). Paul shifts the focus to events in Jerusalem. He maneuvers nimbly in the narrative as he seeks to appeal to the authority of the church leaders in Jerusalem without portraying himself as a lesser apostle. On one hand he displays that the leaders in Jerusalem affirmed the message he preached and his mission to the Gentiles. On the other hand, in various ways, he portrays himself as at the same level of these esteemed leaders.

What Paul describes in these verses has many similarities with the Jerusalem council portrayed in Acts 15:1-35. Although some argue he could instead be referring to a Jerusalem visit mentioned in Acts 11:30, I think the relationship with Acts 15 is more likely. The truth is we cannot know for sure and what we learn from the section does not depend on settling on one or the other.

Continuing with the theme of the narrative in the above section Paul makes clear that he did not go to Jerusalem because others with more authority called him. Rather Paul responded to a revelation. It could be that Paul himself received this revelation directly from God, but it is important to remember that Paul received revelation from God in various ways and through others (for example, see: Acts 9:1-19; 11:28; 13:2; 16:6-9; 18:9-10; 20:22-23; 22:17-21; 27:23-24; 2 Corinthians 12:2-4). With Acts 13:2-3 and Acts 15:2-3, and the emphasis on community in Galatians, it is best that we do not think of this an individual action organized and carried out by Paul. A community of Christians sent Paul, Barnabas, and Titus.

Including Titus in the group would appear to be a deliberate and provocative act. He was an uncircumcised Greek (2:1, 3) who apparently had converted in response to Paul's proclamation of the gospel (Titus1:4). His appearance at the gathering directly confronted the Jerusalem church leaders with the issue of Gentile converts. They did not have the luxury of a theoretical discussion about something happening elsewhere in the world. The presence of Titus as an individual convert was important, but so too was the group Paul, Barnabas, and Titus. They symbolized the community that was fruit of God's action—a community in which circumcision was not a barrier to communion. Titus did not have to do what the agitators insisted upon. He did not have to start living like a Jew in order to be part of the Christian community. The composition of the delegation was a flesh and blood testimony of the truth of the gospel (2:5).

Let us imagine ourselves sitting beside Gentile believers in Galatia listening to this section of the letter. What would have stood out to them? First of all, Paul states that at the root of the problem were "false believers" who sought to enslave them (2:4). The similarity with Paul's comment about a "different gospel" (1:6-7) and the other missionaries in Galatia would have caught their attention. Secondly, the Galatians would have taken note that in relation to the very issue in debate, circumcision, the leaders of the church had sided with Paul and affirmed the gospel he preached. Third, they would have observed that for Paul this was not a side issue, it was central to the race he was running (2:2). Finally, in case they had not made the connection, Paul makes it explicit, what was decided in Jerusalem had direct implications for them. It had preserved the truth of the gospel *for them* (2:5).

It is not clear if these false believers had infiltrated the meeting in Jerusalem or if they had earlier gone and infiltrated the church in Antioch where Jews and Gentiles worshiped together. What is clear is that Paul considered it a serious issue—an attack on the truth of the gospel (2:5). The words "truth of the gospel" may first bring to mind correct information in contrast to a false articulation of the content of the gospel. Certainly that is a concern of Paul's, but as we will explore in more detail in relation to Galatians 2:14, when Paul uses the phrase "truth of the gospel" he is referring to a lived reality that flows from an encounter with Jesus Christ that has rescued a community of believers from the present evil age.

The truth of the gospel is closely related to freedom. If the infiltrators had been successful Paul states it would have undermined their freedom and led to enslavement (2:4). This is the first time in the letter that Paul uses "freedom" and "slavery" as an antithetical pair. The pair will appear as a major theme in the letter (2:4; 3:28; 4:1-11;4:21-5:1; 5:13). Richard Hays observes that is noteworthy "that in the first appearance of these words, 'freedom' refers to the unqualified association of Jewish and Gentile Christians, while 'enslavement' refers to the attempted imposition of circumcision on Gentile believers" (Hays 2000, 225). Therefore, we note that for Paul the "truth of the gospel" and "freedom in Christ" have significance not only for the individual, since both also have a communal character. To be centered in Christ has implications for interpersonal relations. The truth of the gospel manifests itself in a group centered on Christ which is, therefore, freed from the enslaving power of bounded group religiosity and its line-drawing division between insiders and outsiders.

In the final verses in this narrative section where Paul communicates that the leaders added nothing to his message and affirmed his missionary work among the Gentiles, he continues to keep God's action as central and foundational. Note that he does not say they gathered, negotiated, and decided; rather they *recognized.*

They recognized God's actions: God entrusting Paul with the task of preaching the gospel to the uncircumcised, God entrusting Peter with the task of preaching the gospel to the circumcised (2:7), God at work in both Peter and Paul (2:8), God giving grace to Paul (2:9). Just as the inclusion of Titus powerfully communicated symbolically, so too Paul includes in the narrative the symbolic act of the pillars of the church affirming Paul and Barnabas, and their message and mission, through giving them "the right hand of fellowship" (2:9).

It is likely that Paul's next words, "All they asked was…" (2:10), grabbed the attention of the Galatians. I imagine them leaning in with expectation, perhaps thinking, "Apparently the other missionaries were not totally wrong, there are some practices of the Jews that we do need to take up." What would they have thought when Paul finished the sentence? The Jerusalem leaders did not mention a religious ritual or rule that a bounded church could use to define who belonged to the group. The one thing they asked was to "continue to remember the poor."

Rather than take this request as a general imperative, many have interpreted it as a specific petition to send aid for the poor in the Jerusalem church in a time of need. This interpretation implies that if there had not been great need the leaders would not have said anything to Paul about aiding the poor. Rather than communicating a sense of call to all churches to have a continual concern for the impoverished in their congregations and for their needy neighbors, this interpretation can imply that the call to help the poor applies only in moments of exceptional crisis. Reading it this way turns the phrase into an add-on, not central to the meeting in Jerusalem or the letter itself.

Bruce W. Longenecker argues that this is not the best interpretation. Although it is common today, Longenecker points out that all of the written comments on this text from the first three centuries interpret it in a global and general way. None understood it as a specific petition related to the church in Jerusalem (Longenecker 2010, 161–66). Of course we know that Paul did in fact collect aid for the poor in the Jerusalem church (Romans 15:25-31; 1 Corinthians16:1-4; 2 Corinthians 8:1-9:15). Collecting an offering for the poor in Jerusalem is certainly included in remembering the poor, but there is no clear basis in this verse to limit the phrase "remembering the poor" to only that. In Paul's letters talk of aiding the needy is not limited to the poor in Jerusalem, and he mentions the theme repeatedly—including in this very letter (Galatians 5:13-15; 6:2; 6:9-10; Romans 12:13-16; 1 Corinthians 11:17-34; 2 Corinthians 9:13; Ephesians 4:28, 1 Thessalonians 5:14-15; 2 Thessalonians 3:16-13; 1 Timothy 5:3, 16; 6:17-18; Titus 3:14). This points to the reality that aiding the poor, in a general way, is something Paul was "eager to do" (2:10), and eager to exhort other followers of Jesus to do.

If one mistake is to limit the exhortation to remember the poor only to a case of exceptional need, Ryan Schellenberg exposes another common error, which is to think of Paul's calls to generosity as directed only to those with significant economic means. Certainly his exhortations do include a call to those with wealth to share with those in need, but there were very few wealthy people in early churches. Rather than imagining these words as being for just a few Christians, Schellenberg argues convincingly that Paul called all Christians to generosity. When Paul exhorts believers to "share with the Lord's people in need" (Romans 12:13; Galatians 6:6, 10) he is likely using the term "share" in the sense of reciprocal exchange. Even the poor, those with little resources, often share from the little they have with others in their kinship circle in even greater need. They do so with the expectation they will likewise be aided in a time of need. Paul did not invent this idea, for poor people did this then as they do today (Schellenberg 2018). What was radical about Paul's calls to generosity and the Jerusalem leaders' call to remember the poor was the redefinition of the community of sharing. Rather than one's present kinship group, it included all those following Jesus, even those in another city. This required faith and trust. To give to others when one is already poor means putting faith in God's provision (2 Corinthians 9:8f; Philippians 4:19).

To read this exhortation to remember the poor as a general call to all Christians, rather than a specific emergency appeal to wealthy Christians, has clear implications for followers of Jesus at that time and for us today. It does, however, leave us with the question, why did the Jerusalem leaders pick this one thing to mention and why does Paul include it in his letter? Perhaps the simplest answer is, it was a theme of great importance to them. If the James mentioned here is the same one who wrote the epistle of James, then that epistle, with its strong emphasis on aiding the needy, justice for the poor, and avoiding favoritism, affirms the importance of the theme for him. As we observe in Acts, this commitment to help the poor flowed from following Jesus and a movement of the Holy Spirit. It also has deep roots in the Old Testament. Perhaps the Jerusalem leaders were thinking something like, "Yes, we recognize that Gentiles do not need to become circumcised and live like Jews in order to be part of the community of Jesus followers, but there are things from our Jewish laws and traditions which still are important—like helping the poor."

In terms of this commentary, we might say that while they did not impose circumcision in a bounded group way, this does not mean they were not concerned about distinctives and group identity. A fuzzy church erases lines and loses a sense of group identity. A centered church erases lines and reorients people toward a center that will lead to behavior that distinguishes the groups from others and builds a sense of identity. The Jerusalem leaders were willing to let go of using Jewish "works of the law" (2:16) in a bounded way, but they desired that churches with Gentile believers would still be distinct from other groups, including by helping the poor in a way that went beyond what others in society did. Yet it is not just swapping one means of identity distinction for another. Giving to others in need does more than simply make Jesus followers distinct from others. Developing networks of sharing and mutual support builds community. Those actions will deepen communal bonds.

Paul accomplishes a number of things by including this exhortation to help the poor. First is the power of what is not said. The Jerusalem leaders did not emphasize circumcision as the agitators were doing. Second, it is one of many ways in the letter that Paul communicates the importance of the communal aspect of following Jesus. Third, including this exhortation contributes to an important theme in the letter: Christ frees believers from the slavery of religion and frees them for service. The actions of the false believers in Jerusalem and the agitators in Galatia had a bounded character and produced slavery and division. In contrast, God's action through Jesus that Paul proclaimed produced actions of solidarity between groups of people previously alienated from each other.

Thinking of this narrative section as a whole we observe that, although the other missionaries had not likely claimed to have such a strong and direct affirmation from the pillars of the Jerusalem church, they probably did highlight their connections to Jerusalem and the Jewish core of the Christian movement as a way of validating their teaching. Through this narrative Paul has associated the agitators with the "false believers" group and highlighted that at a particular moment the leaders in Jerusalem had intentionally and explicitly affirmed Paul's position over that of the agitators.

Implications of the Text for Today

Broaden our concept of the gospel. We observed that Paul advanced beyond others in Judaism. He does not recount being burdened by guilt for falling short. If not saved from a feeling of guilt what was Paul saved from? Based on this narrative we can say through Jesus he was saved from a religious distortion of God's law. He was saved from bounded group religiosity that considered insiders as superior to others and led to violent persecution of those on the wrong side of the lines drawn. Paul's narrative invites us to reflect on ways we and others we know might need rescuing from religious distortion of God's ways today. Religion, however, is not the only force in society that leads people to grasp for merit and status by putting others down. What are other forces that the gospel of Jesus Christ will liberate people from today?

Let us be centered like Paul rather than fuzzy. Religion and other systems of evaluation and stratification do produce discrimination, exclusion, shame, and violence—in Paul's day and today. As we observed in chapter one, a common solution in contemporary society is to erase the lines used as a basis of evaluation. There is logic to that. It will lessen the problems listed, but it also will lessen a clear call to positive actions and undercut a sense of calling and motivation to positive change—individually and as a group. Paul erases lines, but he replaces them with a center that includes a clear call to actions like remembering the poor and a clear confrontation of judgmentalism. For Paul freedom from the negatives of bounded group religiosity comes not from moral relativism, but from God's liberating action through Jesus Christ.

Seek dialogue. Paul, Barnabas, and Titus went to Jerusalem in response to a revelation from God. This shows us that God values unity in mission. It is important to note that Paul obeyed the revelation and went to Jerusalem. Many in the church opt to avoid or ignore conflict, others take the easier option of division rather than the work of dialogue. Paul could have stayed where he was thinking it was not worth the trouble to seek unity with the conservative and traditional leadership in Jerusalem. He went, not to attack as he would have done earlier in life, but to dialogue. Centered on Jesus let us follow Paul's model of obedience to God and seek dialogue and communion with those we differ with.

Holistic mission. In this narrative we observe emphasis on including the excluded and practicing unity in Christ rather than cultural or religious differences (1:13-21; 2:4-5); an emphasis on preaching the gospel of Jesus Christ (1:16; 2:7); and an emphasis on aiding the poor (2:10). If we only focus on evangelism we will not be practicing the mission Paul describes in this section. If we only focus on people's physical needs we also will not be practicing the mission observed in this narrative. It is not, however, just that Paul's ministry is holistic because it includes spiritual and physical elements. It is broader and deeper than that. For instance in a holistic mission centered on Jesus the poor will be invited into the family of faith as brothers and sisters. Therefore it will not just be a paternalistic activity of those with more helping those with less. Rather it will be a community of mutual sharing and interdependence. Part of what it means to aid the poor is to change the societal dynamic between the poor and others. A church practicing a holistic mission centered on Jesus can change that dynamic.

Personal Response

- Paul's encounter with God certainly included internal transformation, yet Richard Hays exhorts us to not dwell only on the internal, but "dwell, instead, on God's act of seizing us and empowering us for tasks we never could have imagined" (Hays 2000, 220). What might God be calling you to?

- What part of Paul's narrative in this chapter most challenges you? What part gives you the most hope?

- Take a moment and reflect on experiences of dialogue you have experienced in times of church conflict? What can you learn from Paul's experience and your own?

- Do you feel more pull toward the bounded approach of the false brethren, or toward the fuzzy approach of many today? How does this chapter challenge you?

- When you read biblical texts about caring for the poor do you tend to interpret that as a special command specific to the original audience, as a special directive to wealthy Christians, or maybe as a paternalistic one-way act? What might it look like in your community to expand your kinship group—to share reciprocally with the poor?

CHAPTER FIVE

Inclusion Through Jesus

The Text: Galatians 2:11-16

[11] *When Cephas came to Antioch, I opposed him to his face, because he stood condemned.* [12] *For before certain men came from James, he used to eat with the Gentiles. But when they arrived, he began to draw back and separate himself from the Gentiles because he was afraid of those who belonged to the circumcision group.* [13] *The other Jews joined him in his hypocrisy, so that by their hypocrisy even Barnabas was led astray.*

[14] *When I saw that they were not acting in line with the truth of the gospel, I said to Cephas in front of them all, "You are a Jew, yet you live like a Gentile and not like a Jew. How is it, then, that you force Gentiles to follow Jewish customs?*

[15] *"We who are Jews by birth and not sinful Gentiles* [16] *know that a person is not justified by the works of the law, but through the faithfulness of Jesus Christ. So we, too, have put our faith in Christ Jesus that we may be justified*

on the basis of the faithfulness of[a] *Christ and not by the works of the law,*
because by the works of the law no one will be justified.

---

a. The NIV translation of 2:16 is "by faith in Jesus Christ . . . justified by faith in Christ"
    but in the footnotes it states "Or 'but through the faithfulness of . . . justified on the
    basis of the faithfulness of.'" I have opted to use the alternative translation in the text.
    See further explanation in the "Text Explained" section.

The Flow and Form of the Text

In this section Paul continues writing in narrative form. This,
however, is definitely a different chapter in the story. We have a
scene change from Jerusalem to Antioch and a plot change from
a scene of unity and agreement to one of division. Some of the
characters—Paul, Barnabas, Peter (Cephas), and James—remain
the same. Paul first describes the unified table fellowship in
Antioch—Gentile Christians and Jewish Christians, including
Peter. He then recounts the tragic rupture of that unified table and
Peter's role in it. The final part of the Antioch narrative focuses
on Paul confronting Peter for what he had done.

As we read this section and immerse ourselves in the story of
what happened in Antioch let us not forget about Galatia. It is a
story about Antioch told to the Galatians. They would have quickly
noted the similarity between the table-dividers in Antioch and the
perspectives of the agitators in Galatia. The story concretely warns
the Galatians of the fruit of the other missionaries' teaching. The
story is rich with statements on discipleship and theology, told
with purpose. Paul's words to Peter also confront the agitators and
are stated for the benefit and knowledge of the Gentile Christians
receiving the letter. With theological discourse rooted in a real-life
setting, Paul begins the theological argument that will continue
in the chapters ahead. Keep the divided communion table and the

issue of who can join in table fellowship in mind as you read the theological statements of the latter part of the section.

The Text Explained

Tables divided by bounded religiosity versus centered living out of the truth of the gospel (2:11-14a). "When Cephas came to Antioch, I opposed him to his face, because he stood condemned" (2:11). (Cephas is Aramaic for rock, just as Peter is derived from the Greek word for rock.) This sentence is often divided from the previous one by a section title in our Bibles or, in the case of this book, is in a completely different chapter than the previous sentence. The recipients of this letter, however, heard this line right after Paul's words about fellowship and agreement between Paul and James, John and Cephas/Peter. Now just two verses later Paul writes of confronting Peter—a shocking twist in the narrative.

In Greek the connection to the previous verses and the contrast to them is even clearer. The sentence starts with "but"—"But when Cephas. . . ." Why did Paul begin the Antioch narrative with such a direct and bold statement about opposing Peter? In part, it continues the back and forth dance Paul has done since the first chapter—on one hand communicating that the Jerusalem leaders support him and on the other downplaying their importance and his relationship with them. His authority is from God. It also lets us, and the listeners in Galatia, know that what is coming was of such import that he confronted Peter about it. This communicates that if even Peter could get off track, then the other missionaries might also be off track, regardless of their connections to Jerusalem.

We have already explored the actual happenings in Antioch in the first chapter of this book. (You may want to review that part of chapter one.) We will pick up the story in verse 14 with Paul addressing Peter. We will continue to use the lenses of honor-shame dynamic and bounded-set and centered-set as we read and interpret these verses. One way of accentuating the centered character of Paul's response to Peter is to ask: If Paul operated from a bounded-set or fuzzy-set perspective, what would he have done? I encourage you to stop and think about that for a few minutes before reading some possibilities I imagine.

If Paul practiced a fuzzy approach he likely would not have said anything to Peter. He might disagree with Peter's actions and would likely be upset at Peter's bounded actions and how they impacted the Galatian Christians. Yet in a fuzzy-church paradigm he would have no basis on which to confront Peter, and, of course, would not want to risk making Peter feel bad.

If Paul practiced a bounded approach he likely would have entered into a discussion about "right rules." He would not critique the action of drawing lines, but argue about the content of the lines. He probably would pressure Peter through shaming words and accusing looks as the visitors from Jerusalem had done, except to communicate the opposite—that to be a true Christian Peter needed to eat *with* the Gentiles. If he did not, Peter would not be able to eat at the *true* table of Jesus. A bounded set mentality would lead to two dueling tables, each confident in their in-group status as the people who were right.

Paul's centered approach is immediately evident in verse 14. Paul is not fuzzy; he confronts Peter. He also is not bounded. A centered approach evaluates orientation (toward the center or away from it) and evaluates movement (getting closer or moving away from the center). We sense the focus on orientation and movement in Paul's statement: "they were not acting in line with the truth of the gospel" (2:14). It is especially apparent if we look at the Greek word translated as "acting" It is "*orthopodeō.*" We see its relation to our words "orthodox" and "podiatrist." Literally, it is right walking. John Barclay offers this translation of the phrase: "not walking straight in line with the truth of the good news" (Barclay 2015, 367). Paul is saying to Peter, "You are not heading toward the center."

We will explore the centered approach of loving confrontation in more depth when we reflect on Galatians 6:1 but will quickly underline one important characteristic we observe here. Bounded churches use shame to influence behavior. Certainly this was a moment of shame for Peter; yet Paul's purpose is not to shame and exclude Peter so Paul can feel secure and superior on the right side of the line. In contrast to the shaming actions of a bounded church, Paul's intent is restorative. For the good of Peter and for the good of community, Paul confronts Peter with the intent of reorienting back to the way of Jesus.

What do you think of when you hear the phrase "truth of the gospel"? I tend to think of a correct theological articulation of the gospel. If we read this phrase with image #1 from chapter one in mind—individuals with a burden of guilt confused about works and grace—then we easily imagine that when Paul wrote "truth of the gospel" he had in mind correct doctrinal information about works and grace. But that does not match the context. There is nothing in the preceding verses about Peter, or anyone else, stating salvation is by works; nor is there any mention of guilt. And Paul did not accuse Peter of not believing the truth of the gospel or of misstating the truth of the gospel. Rather Paul focused on actions not matching up with the truth of the gospel.

What happens, however, if we read the phrase with image #2 from chapter one in mind? It leads us to think that the rupture of table fellowship is the opposite of the truth of gospel. For Paul the truth of the gospel is not just correct information about salvation through Jesus Christ, it is also a lived out reality that flows from an encounter with Jesus who has freed them from the present evil age (1:4). Paul presents an image that illustrates the truth of the gospel: a group of people, Jews and Gentiles, united by Jesus Christ and eating at the same table. Paul certainly would affirm a doctrinal statement of salvation by grace, but the truth of the gospel is not only a doctrine, it is also a social reality.

We must remember that the agitators, Peter, and the visitors from Jerusalem believed in and taught the truth of the gospel in the first sense—correct information about salvation through grace. But their actions dividing the united table had the character of human religion focused on human behavior. They drew religious lines of division that distinguished between those truly belonging to the people of God and outsiders who did not have a seat at the table. Their identity rested in the lines they drew, not in a relationship centered on Jesus. They had some doctrinal information correct, but they did not live out the truth of the gospel.

Justified by the faithfulness of Jesus Christ (2:14b-16). We now turn to what Paul said to Peter when he confronted him. Paul first points out something that everyone knew, and what made this all the more tragic and hypocritical. Peter had led the way in including Gentile believers in the fellowship. Paul's statement about forcing Jewish customs on Gentile believers underscores what we just observed about what Paul is thinking when he confronts Peter and mentions truth of the gospel. The issue is bounded group religiosity expressed as religious-cultural imperialism.

Paul then switches from "you" singular, addressing Peter individually, to "we." This communicates that he is reminding Peter, in what follows, of something they both affirm. The "we" also would have included the other Jewish believers present in

Antioch, and the agitators in Galatians listening to the letter. It is best to think of "sinful Gentiles" being in quotation marks, as some Bible translations do, first to communicate that Paul is saying this with irony, and second that he is probably borrowing the language of the Jerusalem visitors and the agitators. His point is not to put the Gentiles down, rather to set up what comes next: even those Christians who put themselves on the right side of the lines they have drawn still affirm they are justified through Jesus Christ, not through their religious practices.

The phrase "justified by faith" (2:16) is so familiar to many we might assume it does not need further explanation. We might be tempted to simply state what appears to be the obvious and clear meaning of the verse: we are declared innocent of guilt through faith in Jesus, not because of works we have done. Having stated this meaning we could affirm its importance and quickly move on to the next verse. We are going to do exactly the opposite, however. We will spend more time with this verse than any other verse in the book, not because it is the most complex or confusing verse in the letter, but because we need to peel off quite a few layers of paint in order to see something closer to what Paul actually painted. We will work to read it in line with image #2 from chapter one (the table at Antioch) rather than image #1 (individual struggling with guilt). So, get out your paint scrapers as we begin by looking at one key word from the verse: "justified."

Significant Concept: Justification

A common image of justification is an individual standing before a judge and the judge pronouncing that person not guilty. Moving into the theological realm, the word "justification" leads many Christians to imagine God adjusting an individual's legal record in heaven—moving that person's name into the not-guilty column because of the cross of Christ. The essence of this view of justification is captured well by the simple definition commonly taught in Sunday School: to be justified means that because of Christ, God can look at me *just as if* I had never sinned. This understanding of justification can be seen in the Living Bible's rendering of Romans 3:24. Instead of using the word "justified" it says: "God declares us 'not guilty' of offending him."

If we are thinking about Luther's experience when we read Galatians 2:16 this understanding fits well. Luther was freed from his burden of guilt by trusting in Jesus rather than his works. But Paul spoke these words in Antioch to Peter. The conflict was about who can eat together. Why in the midst of that discussion of circumcision, Jewish practices, and table fellowship would Paul suddenly start talking to Peter about being declared not guilty? Picture the scene if we put this understanding of justification in Paul's mouth. Deeply disturbed, he confronts Peter, "Why this hypocrisy?! Why have you pulled away from table fellowship with these Gentile believers? You are not living in line with the truth of the gospel! You know we are declared not guilty by trusting the work of Jesus!" Feel the incongruity of the last phrase? Why would he say that in this context? Perhaps the answer to those questions is that Paul meant something different by the word "justified." We will first look at how just/justice/justified is understood from a Western legal understanding and then from a Hebraic understanding. Would Paul's culture and Jewish scriptures, what we call the Old Testament, have led him to understand this word differently than the Western legal understanding that influences the just-as-if-I-had-never-sinned definition?

In modern Western legal systems an impersonal code of laws provides the means for the judge to weigh the case. The central questions are: is the person guilty of breaking the law? What punishment do they deserve? One is considered innocent or guilty, just or unjust, depending upon how they measure up against the abstract ideal or code. Justice is thought of as following the procedures fairly and the guilty party getting the punishment stipulated by the law. Crimes have victims, yet in criminal cases the central issue is how the accused measures up against the legal code, not making things right with the victim. With this understanding of justice we quite naturally think that for God to justify an individual is to pronounce them as "not guilty"—that is, to view the person as if they had met the standard of the justice.

The Hebraic concept of justice seen in the Old Testament has a relational foundation. The basis of judgment is how faithful one is to agreements, obligations, or covenants with other people and with God. To act justly is to be faithful to the people one is committed to by agreement or covenant. The relationship, not an impersonal law, is central. Of course there are laws in the Old Testament, but the laws are relational in the sense that God gave them within a covenant relationship as an expression of God's intention for life and community within Israel. Therefore, a person would be seen as just by God if they lived in a way that demonstrated faithfulness to commitments to others and to Israel's covenant with God.

Before we look at some biblical texts, an important note on language. In English Bibles, the same word is translated at times as "justice" and at times as "righteousness." Other languages use the one word "justice" throughout. In this section I will use "justice" for ease of understanding. If you want to check this out yourself look at a Bible verse that has "righteous" in English, like Matthew 6:33, and then look at the verse in another language you know. Matthew 6:33 and Galatians 2:16 have the same Greek root word.

The contrast between the Hebrew relational sense of justice and our abstract concept of justice is striking at times. Imagine if today I stood before a judge, admitted my guilt, and then appealed to the judge's sense of justice: "Please your honor, I appeal to your sense of justice. Do not send me to jail." You would conclude I was not thinking straight. It would be the equivalent of asking the judge to give me the punishment the law demands. If I wanted to avoid punishment I would not plead for justice, I would appeal to the judge's sense of mercy. Yet David does just what would seem ludicrous in a Western court. He pleads, "Lord, hear my prayer, listen to my cry for mercy; in your faithfulness and justice come to my relief. Do not bring your servant into judgment, for no one living is just before you" (Psalm 143:1-2, my adaptation of NIV). He admits that he is not just/righteous, but he not only appeals to God's mercy, but also God's justice/righteousness—asking God to not punish him and help him in his trouble (143: 2-3, 11). Is David not thinking straight? Actually his logic is sound. For him the word "justice" means something different. According to the Hebrew concept of justice David's request for God to act justly makes perfect sense. David's concept of justice includes a strong emphasis on faithfulness. David asks God to be just, faithful to God's pact of love with David, even though David has not acted faithfully/justly. In essence he is saying, "God I have not kept my covenant with you, but please keep your covenant with me." (For a similar example see Daniel 9:4-19.)

An example from the New Testament clearly displays a similar Hebraic perspective on justice. Before he was told otherwise by an angel, Joseph naturally assumed that Mary had sex with another man. According to the law she should be stoned (Deuteronomy 22:23-24). Matthew writes that because Joseph was a "just man," he was going to divorce her quietly rather than expose her publicly

(Matthew 1:19 KJV). From a Western perspective, Joseph is not being just. He is intentionally disregarding the law. Clearly Matthew is using the term "just" to mean something other than strictly following the legal code. Out of deep loyalty and respect for Mary, Joseph sought a way to circumvent the law, rectify the situation, and save her. Matthew considered this a just action, an illogical statement from a Western legal perspective.

As in the Western judicial context, in the relational justice context of the Old Testament the word "justice" is associated with terms like "law" and "punishment." But, as we observed in Psalm 143, many times in the Old Testament "justice" is also related to words like "faithfulness," "mercy," and "salvation" (for example: Isaiah 45:20-25, Isaiah 51:4-8, Psalm 40:9-11, and Psalm 98:1-3). To relate these words with justice does not makes sense if we think of justice from the Western perspective. But it does from a Hebraic perspective. God is just because God is totally faithful to his promises and covenants and works to rectify, to make things right. Similarly a Jewish person would be seen as just by God if they live in a way that demonstrates faithfulness to Israel's covenant with God.

It is important to note that the relational concept of justice has a strong social or communitarian emphasis. The covenant and the law are not focused just on the behavior of individuals but on forming a people.

So, from scripture and his Hebraic cultural background Paul, likely would have understood the verb "to justify" to include the sense of declaring innocent, but also a sense of straightening out or restoring relationships that have been twisted or broken. We see this combination of language in Romans 5:8-10. Sinners are equated to God's enemies, and justified and reconciled are used in a parallel way. In the Hebraic sense, to be just would mean to be in proper covenant relationship. Therefore, Richard Hays argues that when we see Paul using the words justice or justified we should think "primarily in terms of the covenant relationship to God and membership within the covenant community" (Hays 1992, 1131). N. T. Wright similarly suggests the meaning, "covenant membership" or "covenant status" (Wright 1991, 201).

In Galatians, to be justified is not simply to be declared not guilty of having broken laws, or to be placed in proper relationship with standards recorded in an impersonal code. To be justified is to be placed in proper relationship to God—to be made a full participant in the community of God's people. The individualistic image of a heavenly ledger book falls short. As Richard Hays states:

> There is no question here of a legal fiction whereby God juggles his heavenly account books and pretends not to notice human sin. The legal language points rather to the formal inclusion of those who were once "not my people" in a concrete historical community of the "sons of the living God" (Rom. 9:25-26). (Justification is only one of the metaphors that Paul can use to describe this act of inclusion by grace; elsewhere he can speak, for example, of "adoption," as in Gal. 4:5 and Rom. 8:15) (Hays 1992, 1131–32).

A Western understanding of justification leaves us asking, "What does an individual's burden of guilt have to do with the split tables at Antioch?" In contrast, the Hebraic understanding of justification is fully pertinent to the communal questions about who belongs at the table.

The Hebrew concept of justice and the way Paul's justification language relates to the Antioch incident indicate that Paul has a corporate and social concept of justification that centers on relationship and covenant status or inclusion in the people of God.

To think of justification as inclusion in the people of God, or membership in the covenant community, helps us feel the corporate aspect of the word. Nevertheless, it is important to remember that in Galatians 2:16 Paul doesn't write the word "justification" but "to be justified." As stated above, from the relational Hebraic perspective the verb "to justify" has a sense of making right or straightening out or restoring relationships that have been twisted or broken. Now Paul affirms that he, Peter and the other Jewish Christians agree that this straightening out of relationship comes through Jesus.

To summarize, both the context of where Paul used the word and the way he likely understood the word point to a meaning other than "declared as not guilty." That is not to say, however, that Luther or that definition are totally wrong. To be released from guilt is *part* of what the word "justified" means in Galatians. But it means much more than that. To say that someone is justified also carries a sense of inclusion within the community of faith and a straightening or rectifying of relations with God and others in the people of God. In contrast to a Western understanding, the Hebraic understanding includes both a vertical (with God) as well as horizontal (with others) element, both an individual as well as communal character.

To scrape away the Western legal understanding of justice that has been painted over Paul's use of the word "justified" is a major step, but the very next words in the verse, "works of the law," require significant scraping work as well.

Significant Concept: Works of the Law

Paul states that a person is not justified by "the works of the law" (2:16). How is this understood if read through the lens of Luther's experience (chapter one) and the stereotype of the agitators (chapter two)? People have commonly understood Paul as saying that no one can obtain salvation by obeying the Jewish laws, specifically, and in a more general way by works or human effort. The "judge" will always pronounce a guilty verdict because humans will always fall short of the standard. Although that may ring true for what Luther needed—a correction of his misguided efforts of seeking peace with God—it does not actually line up with the Old Testament or Jewish teaching in Paul's time. As we observed in chapter two, Jews at the time of Paul did not teach that someone would be saved by keeping all of the law. As Paul will make clear later in the letter (3:17), the law came after the covenant. It was not given as precondition. God did not say, "if you obey all these laws you will become my people." The law itself assumed people would not obey it perfectly. It provided a means for people to become reconciled with God after they had sinned or broken a law. If "works of the law" is not a general statement about human efforts to earn God's approval and salvation, what did Paul mean by the phrase?

Some scholars have argued that by "works of the law" Paul is referring primarily to practices (such as circumcision, dietary laws, and Sabbath observance) that Jewish people used to demonstrate one was a "good Jew" and to separate and distinguish themselves from Gentiles. Other scholars maintain that Paul was referring to all of the laws recorded in the Old Testament, and they often lean toward the salvation-not-by-works interpretation described above. James D. G. Dunn has done extensive work on this issue to demonstrate that Jews at the time did use this phrase as shorthand to refer especially to Jewish identity practices like circumcision and dietary laws. Dunn clarifies that to link "works of the law" to a few distinction-maintaining practices is not to imply that Jews at the time thought they only had to keep this limited list of commandments and not all the law. Rather, to connect the phrase especially to circumcision and dietary laws highlights the relationship between "works of the law" and what I call bounded group religiosity.

It is important to note that Dunn, and others, are not simply saying, "This emphasis and this shorthand had always been true." Rather, they point out that in that time period there was a heightened emphasis given to the function of circumcision and food laws as marks of distinction (See for instance 1 Maccabees 1:60-63). It is not, however, that we lean on outside information to interpret the phrase in this way in Galatians. The clues of what Paul had in mind when he wrote "a person is not justified by the works of the law" are within the text itself.

An important clue appears a few lines earlier. Paul had said to Peter, "How is it, then, that you force Gentiles to follow Jewish customs?" (2:14) or as many other versions translate it, "force Gentiles to live like Jews." If we read verse 16 as continuing the flow of logic started in verse 14, we would assume Paul has the same thing in mind and is communicating to Peter that they know they are not justified by living like a Jew and following Jewish customs. Or, making the point in the opposite way, in verse 14 Paul does not say to Peter, "How is it, then, that you tell Gentiles they must obey all of the law in order to be saved." Therefore, it is unlikely that is what he meant by "works of the law" a couple lines later.

The second significant clue is the point of disagreement in Antioch (and in Jerusalem [2:1-10] and Galatia as well). The problem in Antioch is that the visitors from Jerusalem refused to share table fellowship with the uncircumcised and those who did not adhere to Jewish dietary laws. So, when Paul says "works of the law" in that context, specific practices at the center of the disagreement must have been at the forefront of everyone's mind. As Dunn writes, "Whatever else he had in mind when he wrote 'works of the law' in 2;16, Paul certainly had in mind circumcision and food laws" (Dunn 2008, 417).

Dunn looks even deeper into the letter and Paul's experience to sharpen our understanding of Paul's use of this phrase.

> The "works of the law" which Paul had particularly in mind were rules which, unless embraced by Gentiles, should prevent full acceptance of these Gentiles. . . . They marked out the distinction between the chosen nation and all others. . . . Paul in or as a result of his conversion reacted particularly against Jewish exclusivism, . . .against what had become a more and more dominant feature of Jewish belief in the preceding two hundred years—a zeal for the law which treated other Jews as sinners and apostates in effect, and, in extension of the same zeal, regarded Gentiles as "beyond the pale." Paul expresses this in Galatians in describing his conversion as a turning from such zeal to the conviction that he had been called to take the news of God's son to the Gentiles (1:13-16). . . . We should not underestimate the seriousness of the exclusivistic attitude against which Paul now reacted . . . an exclusivistic attitude . . . that leads to exclusivistic conduct. . . . It was that sort of "attitude toward the law" which Paul came to abhor. . . . The

crisis for Paul in these confrontations [in Jerusalem, in Antioch, and with the agitators in Galatia] was occasioned by the outworking of the same old exclusivism within the ranks of believers in Messiah Jesus: uncircumcised, unobservant Gentile believers should be "excluded, regarded as outsiders" (4:17). At Jerusalem and Antioch Paul resisted this policy with the same forthrightness as he had enacted it prior to his conversion. And in 2:16 it is that exclusivism which is encapsulated in one degree or another in the phrase "works of the law.". . . In short, whatever else Gal. 2:16 may mean or be taken to mean, it certainly was intended to warn against "works of the law" as constituting or erecting barriers to the free extension of God's grace to the Gentiles (Dunn 2008, 417–18).

Dunn's interpretation of what Paul meant by "works of the law" coheres with a number of perspectives I have emphasized in this book. 1. The problem in Galatia was not mistaken doctrine and explicit teaching that one is saved by works. 2. Rather, it sprang more from a different conception of God's grace and worthiness. 3. A different understanding of grace combined with bounded group religiosity produced a situation where believers needed to practice certain Jewish customs in order to have the "membership card" that enabled them to be considered truly part of the people of God. 4. Paul wrote the letter with passionate rejection of this line-drawing judgmentalism as counter to the gospel of Jesus Christ and deep concerns for church communities and their unity.

—

Therefore, bringing together what we have seen in the previous two sections I offer this paraphrase of part of Galatians 2:16: "A person is not placed in right relationship with God or included in the covenant community through showing a membership card of ethnic identity or by practicing certain traditions associated with the people of God."

If inclusion within the people of God is not based on observing Jewish practices, what *is* it based on? The answer to that question is the next phrase in the verse. Paul's words in Greek were "*dia pisteos Iēsou Christou*" (2:16). One possible translation is "through the faith of Jesus Christ" or "through Christ's faithfulness" (subjective genitive). The second possibility is "through faith in Jesus Christ" (objective genitive). In the first, Christ is the acting subject. In the second, humans are the acting subject and Christ is the object of their faith. The question becomes: Is a person justified by their faith or by Christ's faithfulness? (This same phrase is repeated later in 2:16 and also in Galatians: 2:20; 3:22, 26, and Romans 3:22, 26; Philippians 3:9.) Most modern translations use the objective genitive—*faith in*. But over the last forty years an increasing number of scholars have argued for the subjective genitive, which is the way the KJV translated it. Some recent translations have opted for "faithfulness of Christ" or have included a footnote that offers it as a possible translation.

Grammatically, either translation is a correct possibility. The translation decision, therefore, leans on one's interpretation of where Paul would most likely put the emphasis. Before explaining why I think "faithfulness of Christ" is the better option, it is important to underscore that the debate is not over whether Paul considered an individual's belief in Christ important. In fact, in the middle of this same verse Paul states, "So, we too, have put our faith in Christ Jesus." (There is no debate about that translation meaning faith in Christ Jesus. It is a different form of the Greek word.) Paul unambiguously affirmed the importance of the act of believing/trusting directed towards Christ as object. The disagreement is not over whether or not he wrote of human faith, rather it is whether he—three times in one verse—wrote of human faith in Jesus, or twice of Christ's faithfulness and once of human faith.

The key question in deciding which translation option is more likely, is to ask, "In this particular setting in Antioch, and Galatia, would Paul want to put more emphasis on human action or God's action?" In a situation where people are being pulled toward what I described in chapter two as a religious orientation, in this letter Paul has repeatedly emphasized God's action. Perhaps the best clue as to how to translate this phrase in Galatians 2:16 is Paul's self-correction in 4:9, where he switches from words of human action to words of God's action. He understood the religious mindset. People assume they need to do something to earn good standing with God. The "faith of/faithfulness of Christ" translation makes this verse read as the anti-religious statement I believe Paul intended it to be. It says that a person is not justified by human actions, nor even human belief, but by God's work through Jesus Christ. Paul then affirms, in the next line, his human faith/trust in Jesus' action. Paul puts his trust in his being justified through Jesus' faithful obedience.

What might that mean? How does Jesus' faithful obedience restore us to right relations with God and others in the covenant People of God? It is most helpful to think about concrete faithfulness and to think of that obedience in the context of God's covenant with Israel. Jesus faithfully obeyed God his father, even to the point of death. He fulfilled the covenant commitments that Israel had not. He kept, in our place, the human side of the covenant.

Prophets in the Old Testament pointed to this possibility of all people benefiting and being pardoned for their covenant failures by one person living justly (Jeremiah 5:1; Is 58:12; Ezekial 22:30-31). As we will explore in the next chapter, we are justified through union with this righteous one's life, death, and resurrection.

Based on the above exploration of what Paul likely had in mind when he said these words to Peter and wrote them to the Galatians, I offer this paraphrase of the full verse (2:16):

> Knowing that a person is not brought into right relationship with God and included within the people of God on the basis of practices that distinguish Jews from others, we also placed our faith in Christ Jesus in order that we might be brought into right relationship with God and included within the people of God on the basis of Christ's faithfulness and not because we comply with Jewish practices, like circumcision and dietary practices, that serve as boundary lines between Jews and others.

Conclusion

As is often the case when scraping off old paint, we spent a lot of time on specific spots or details. As we conclude this chapter I want to take a step back and remind us of where these words to Peter were said and why.

In Antioch Peter bowed to the pressure of bounded group religiosity. His act of separating from the united table in Antioch made clear that a boundary line existed that excluded fellow Christ followers because they did not comply with standards that distinguished Jews from others. Even if he and the others did not state it, their actions implied that a relationship with Jesus was not enough to be part of the family of God. Paul reacted strongly against what Peter did because he saw it as a return to the ways of the "present evil age" and not the new creation produced by God's action through Jesus Christ (1:4, 6:14-15).

Many, including the other missionaries, likely argued that if Gentile believers would take up these Jewish practices it would bring peace and union. But Paul knew it would be a union based on religious uniformity rather than on Jesus. In a bounded group, one's sense of belonging and the group's sense of unity is based on excluding others. Perhaps following the agitators' approach of a Jesus-and gospel would bring temporary unity, but it would communicate a sense of exclusion. Over time it would cause division again. Paul knew that religion is fundamentally divisive and the gospel of Jesus Christ is fundamentally inclusive and unifying.

Some argue that Paul wrote this letter out of concern for individuals confused about salvation, grace, and works. Others argue that Paul wrote out of concern for the community. Observing Paul's passionate response to the split tables at Antioch and reflecting on his likely understanding of justification demonstrates this is a false dichotomy. Paul wrote with concern for both individuals and communities. Justification is experienced individually and an aspect of it is inclusion within the covenant community of God's people. Clearly, Paul confronted Peter because of the impact of his actions on the community. Yet the religious line-drawing actions of Peter impacted individuals. It caused them to experience shame and potentially distorted their understanding of grace and salvation—not because of explicit teaching about works- based salvation, but because of what is communicated implicitly through bounded group religiosity.

Implications of the Text for Today

Work to shift from a Western to a Hebraic understanding of justice and justification. How we conceive of justification has implications way beyond how we will interpret Paul's words to Peter. For instance, imagine someone doing evangelism explaining to the potential convert what it means to be justified. If they take a step of faith and become a Christ follower, that understanding of justification will be part of their foundational understanding of Christianity. Building on a Western understanding of justification will contribute to the convert viewing God as a judge who declares people guilty or innocent, seeing salvation as escaping the guilty penalty, and picturing the church as a collection of individuals who have sought and received the innocent status. The convert would see little connection between their experience of justification/salvation and their ethical living as a disciple of Jesus. In contrast, building on a Hebraic understanding will add other significant features such as:

- God is a judge who also works to rectify and make things right, which means that salvation includes God working actual changes in the person, as well as in relationships;

- there is a strong sense of corporate identity and a view of church as a group of people committed to each other and God;

- and ethics—new ways of living—are integral to the convert's understanding of what it means to be a Christian.

I invite you to reflect on other ways how we think about justification will impact our corporate and individual lives. Let us proclaim this richer, more comprehensive, and compelling gospel.

Here are a few ideas on how to aid in a Hebraic view becoming more common in a church.

- Stop using the image of a judge in a Western courtroom to explain the Pauline concept of justification. Instead, use the image of the divided tables at Antioch, stating that the central questions were: Who can sit at the table of God's people? and What gives them the right to sit there?

- Put aside the image of justification as an adjustment in a heavenly accounting book and God seeing us as if we have not sinned, even though we have. Instead, emphasize the concrete realities possible because of the work of Jesus Christ: restored relationship with God, new relations with others in God's family, freedom from the weight of feeling shame and exclusion, and yes, freedom from guilt.

- Invite people to reflect on times they have suffered the shame and exclusion of being on the wrong side of line and offer the counter example of the possibility, through the gracious action of God through Jesus Christ, of being included and honored as part of the people of God.

Exclude bounded group religiosity, not people. We must do more than teach and proclaim that salvation is by grace—the agitators did that. Like Paul we must recognize that religion distorts the truth of the gospel and confront bounded group religiosity. And, like Paul, confront it not only through shining a light on line-drawing religion but also proclaim the opposite, inclusion through God's gracious work through Jesus Christ. Paul confronted Peter but his objective was not to exclude Peter. Bounded group religiosity excludes; the centered gospel of Jesus reorients and includes.

Follow Paul's example of intentionally using language that underscores God's action. Because of humans' strong religious tendency, we gravitate toward giving importance to our efforts and seeing God's love as conditional. Many people quite explicitly think that their works will determine God's response to them. Christians know they are saved by grace, not works, so they tend not to have that explicit error, but many of us still grab for ways to work to satisfy God and substitute human faith itself as a "work." Therefore, let us follow Paul and undercut this religious tendency by emphasizing God's action and loving initiative.

For example, I encourage you to adapt and borrow these lines—perhaps at communion and in other settings—which Timothy Larsen shares. "I often lead communion in my church. One of the things I say is, 'Come to this table not because you are full of faith, but because he is faithful.' It is that turning to look toward Jesus, 'Lord I believe, help my unbelief,' My confidence is not in myself that I am going to have enough faith, I am just going to look to Jesus" (Larsen 2020).

Erase other lines that divide. I have emphasized the religious nature of the lines of division in Antioch and Galatia. As we have seen in Galatians 4:1–11, Paul identifies the religious factor as well, but in Judaism, religion, culture, and ethnicity were intertwined. Thus, the lines also had an element of cultural imperialism—Jews imposing Jewish ways on non-Jews. Implicit in the couplets that Paul states find unity in Christ (3:28) is the recognition that society often draws lines of division between slaves and free, Jews and Gentiles, men and women. Religious line-drawing sows division and exclusion in churches, but it is not limited to religion. People in churches also grasp for status and security by drawing lines based on ethnicity, gender, political affiliation, social status, income, etc. All of this is counter to the gospel. Let us be self-critical and look for the presence of these lines and erase them.

Personal Response

- What exclusion have you experienced or observed for not having the right identity markers ("works of the law")? What are identity markers you observe on social media or hear others talking about? What are things that others might experience as works-of-the-law identity markers in your church?

- Take a few moments and repeat words describing the Hebraic concept of being justified that Paul proclaimed such as: restoration of relationship, covenant inclusion, making right. What images come to mind? Now place yourself in those images. What does this add to your sense of being justified through Christ? What feelings and thoughts do you have?

- Notice what feelings come to you when you think "I am justified by my faith in Jesus." Now notice what feelings come when you think "I am justified by Jesus's faithfulness." What difference does this shift make in your understanding of God and your relationship to God?

- If you had been in Paul's situation in Antioch, would you have more likely responded to Peter in a bounded, fuzzy, or centered way? What have you learned from observing Paul's centered response?

- Avoiding the judgmental line drawing of bounded group religiosity is of great importance. Let us not, however, run past the positive example of the united table in Antioch that, through Jesus Christ, brought together people who would otherwise not share a meal together. Who are people you would not normally associate with that you could invite to share table fellowship?

CHAPTER SIX

United with Christ

The Text: Galatians 2:17-21

[17] *"But if, in seeking to be justified in Christ, we Jews find ourselves also among the sinners, doesn't that mean that Christ promotes sin? Absolutely not!* [18] *If I rebuild what I destroyed, then I really would be a lawbreaker.*

[19] *"For through the law I died to the law so that I might live for God.* [20] *I have been crucified with Christ and I no longer live, but Christ lives in me. The life I now live in the body, I live by faith in the Son of God, who loved me and gave himself for me.* [21] *I do not set aside the grace of God, for if righteousness could be gained through the law, Christ died for nothing!*

The Flow and Form of the Text

We start a new chapter in this book, but in Galatians we are still in the same section of the text we began in chapter five. In Paul's letter, 2:11-21 is one unit, but because chapter five is already the longest one in the book, I have divided our discussion of the unit into two chapters. As you read this chapter, keep central in your mind the painful division of the communion table in Antioch, as well as Paul's confrontation of Peter. In verse 17 Paul continues to report to the Galatians what he said to Peter. He uses "we Jews" as he has in preceding verses. Chapter 3 in the text of the letter then marks a clear change, for Paul addresses the Galatians directly. Verses 2:19-21 may be words Paul said to Peter, or they may be observations Paul is making to the Galatians, a transitioning to 3:1. In either case, they are connected in content to the previous verses in the unit (2:11-18).

The Text Explained

Competing ideas of what is sinful (2:17-18). Paul has just stated to Peter (2:16) what they both affirm, that they are justified and have a seat at the table of God's family because of Jesus Christ, not because of membership cards based on following certain Jewish practices. Now in verse 17 Paul states something that the visitors from Jerusalem (and perhaps the other missionaries in Galatia) had said in defense of their separating from non-circumcised Christ followers. From their perspective, eating with Gentile sinners means they too would become sinners. (Note the word "sinners" here is the same as in verse 15, and, as there, Paul is using *their* language, not his.) Paul counters their position by stating that to think that way would mean Christ is a servant of sin. If they call it sin for these two groups to be together at one table, then they are calling Jesus Christ's action of erasing of the boundary lines as promoting sin. The word that the *NIV* translates as "promotes" is *diakonos*. Richard Hays writes, "Paul conjures up and then emphatically rejects an absurd image of Christ waiting upon Sin as a personified power; the term *diakonos* ('servant' often used of table servants) links the objection vividly to the scene of Jews and Gentiles eating at one table" (Hays 2000, 241).

Paul accepts that to be justified based on the faithfulness of Jesus will lead him to have communion with people that he previously considered unclean sinners. But he rejects the idea that this is a sinful action. In verse 18 he flips the Jerusalem visitors' accusation on its head. To join them in drawing exclusionary lines based on Jewish distinctives would be returning to his pre-Christ bounded group ways. From the perspective of bounded group religiosity, one's Christian identity is based on guarding the lines and staying within them. Paul says exactly the opposite. It would be a transgression against the way of Christ for him to re-draw religious lines of division.

We have already encountered the phrase "in Christ" or other language of union with Christ (1:16, 22, 2:4) and Paul uses it three times in the verses above. In order to better interpret the remaining verses in this chapter, and other uses of union with Christ in the chapters ahead, we will explore its meaning in depth.

Significant Concept: In Christ

If you ask Christians what is central to Pauline theology many would say justification by faith. It is certainly prominent in Romans 3-5 and in this unit in Galatians, but does justification show up repeatedly? Is it in all his letters? No. It was central in Martin Luther's transformative experience of God's grace which so influences the way many read Paul. Let us take a step back, set Luther aside for a moment, and ask, if not justification, what is a theme that is repeated throughout his writings?

Michael Gorman has drawn my attention to how pervasive the language of union with Christ is in Paul. "For Paul it is as natural to speak about a person or persons being 'in Christ,' . . . as it is for Christians today to refer to themselves as Christians" (Gorman 2019, 4). It is common, but what does it mean? Richard Hays explains, "a mysterious union, a fusion of identities, has occurred, in such a way that Jesus has enacted our destiny in his death and resurrection, and we find ourselves caught up into him, incorporated into his life" (Hays 2014, 214).

Many of us are immersed in an individualistic atomistic culture. It is difficult for us to conceive of things we perceive separate as being united. It is one thing to talk about an individual's actions impacting other individuals, and about Jesus' death and resurrection effecting change that affects me, but it is something else to talk about me as an individual being united with you, and both of us and others being united with Christ in his death and resurrection. Grasping that in a concrete way does not come easily for me. So, for those like me, I want to share—before we turn to Pauline language of union—some examples that might help us.

We do have elements of corporateness in our thinking. For instance, think of the pride and sense of satisfaction you feel when your brother or sister, parent or child has a great success. There is a sense of it being your success too. Or when a family member suffers. They experience the actual pain, but we feel it. If you are a sports fan, recall a time when a team you cheer for won the championship. You're not on the field playing. You might not even be in the stands, but it is your team. You feel united with them in the victory. Think about the Olympics. When someone wins a gold medal, what do people from that country say? "We won!" We are not the competitor, but in a corporate sense the one athlete did it for all, for the whole country. This is one way of thinking about union, one person as representative for others.

Another way of thinking about union is when two or more people become joined together. A team, whether ministry team, business team, sports team can have a strong sense of togetherness. Other examples are the oneness of a married couple, or the union with a person we call a soul mate. Paul and his more collectivist audience would have had an even stronger and more widespread sense of union with others. Even so, perhaps these few examples can aid us as we look at some of Paul's language of participation and union.

The list that follows is representative, not comprehensive. I include it to give a feel for how frequently Paul uses "in Christ" language and the diverse ways he does so.

Romans 6:8 - Now if we died **with Christ,** we believe that we will also **live with him**.

Romans 6:11 - In the same way, count yourselves dead to sin but alive to God **in Christ Jesus.**

Romans 8:1-2 - There is therefore now no condemnation for those who are **in Christ Jesus.** For the law of the Spirit of life **in Christ Jesus** has set you free from the law of sin and of death. (NRSV)

Romans 12:5 - so **in Christ** we, though many, form one body, and each member belongs to all the others.

Romans 16:7-12 - Greet Andronicus and Junia, my relatives who were in prison with me; they are prominent among the apostles, and they were **in Christ** before I was. Greet Ampliatus, my beloved **in the Lord**. Greet Urbanus, our co-worker **in Christ,** and my beloved Stachys. Greet

Apelles, who is approved **in Christ**. Greet those who belong to the family of Aristobulus. Greet my relative Herodion. Greet those **in the Lord** who belong to the family of Narcissus. Greet those workers **in the Lord**, Tryphaena and Tryphosa. Greet the beloved Persis, who has worked hard **in the Lord**. . .

2 Corinthians 5:17-19 - Therefore, if anyone is **in Christ**, the new creation has come: The old has gone, the new is here! All this is from God, who reconciled us to himself through Christ and gave us the ministry of reconcilia-tion: that God was **reconciling the world to himself in Christ,** not counting people's sins against them. And he has committed to us the message of reconciliation.

Galatians 1:22 I was personally unknown to the churches of Judea that are **in Christ.**

Galatians 2:19-20 - For through the law I died to the law so that I might live for God. I have been **crucified with Christ** and I no longer live, but **Christ lives in me.**

Galatians 3:27-28 - for all of you who were **baptized into Christ** have clothed yourselves with Christ. There is neither Jew nor Gentile, neither slave nor free, nor is there male and female, for you are all one **in Christ Jesus.**

Philippians 2:1 - Therefore if you have any encouragement from **being united with Christ,** if any comfort from his love, if any common sharing in the Spirit, if any tenderness and compassion . . .

Colossians 2:10-13 - and **in Christ** you have been brought to fullness. He is the head over every power and authority.

In him you were also circumcised with a circumcision not performed by human hands. Your whole self ruled by the flesh was put off when you were circumcised by Christ, having been buried with him in baptism, in which you were also raised with him through your faith in the working of God, who raised him from the dead. When you were dead in your sins and in the uncircumcision of your flesh, God made you alive with Christ. He forgave us all our sins,

Having looked at a variety of uses of the in-Christ language, let us look at Richard Hays's attempt to categorize this variety (Hays 2008).

1. *Participation as belonging to a family*

For Paul, "belonging to Christ" is the same as being "in Christ." Hays observes that they "might be understood as roughly equivalent metaphors for participation in an extended *family* structure. The passages that speak of belonging to Christ draw upon metaphors related to membership in the extended household of which Christ is pictured as the master" (Hays 2008, 340). What is participation in Christ? It is belonging to the family, to that household of Christ. We see this in Galatians 4:7, to be in Christ is to be no longer a slave, but a son or daughter, made part of the family. Paul also uses the adoption metaphor. Also in Galatians Paul relates being in Christ to being in Abraham's line and participating in Abraham's blessing (3:8, 29). As part of the family, we participate in the privileges, the benefits, and the responsibilities of being in the family, the household of Christ.

2. Participation as political or military solidarity with Christ

Paul also relates "in Christ" to something broader and wider than family. "To be joined with him in baptism is to belong to him and thus to come under his sovereignty. To be 'in Christ,' then, is to enter the sphere of his lordship and thereby to be enlisted on his side in the war against the enslaving power of sin." Remember the name Christ itself is a political term—the anointed one, Messiah. "To be in Christ is to acknowledge his practical Lordship over human lives and to share in his battle, to reclaim sovereignty over the world by yielding our bodies in service of his righteousness" (Hays 2008, 342–43).

3. Participation in the ekklēsia

"For Paul being in Christ was inextricably woven together with his experience of participation in a remarkable new boundary-blurring human community made up of Jews and Gentiles together, a community where Christ's presence was understood to be palpably manifest through the sharing of bread and wine and through the outpouring of the spirit and communal worship" (Hays 2008, 344). In Galatians 3:27-29 Paul links baptism with being clothed in Christ, belonging to Christ and living in the community that erases the boundaries drawn by society to create distinctions that separate. Participation in Christ includes a sense of joining with others and living out what I call a centered church.

4. Participation as living within the Christ story

Living in Christ is living in the narrative of Christ, or what Hays calls narrative participation. Paul summons his hearers and readers into a narrative in which the cross, resurrection, and Parousia (second coming) are the events that define the shape and meaning of history. It is a narrative that calls for response. People either turn away by rejecting the story of Jesus Christ or enter into it and live in light of it. That is, to live in light of what it claims about Jesus. To enter the story is to center life on Jesus. In the words of Hays, those who enter the narrative "learn to see themselves as having been crucified with Christ, so that Christ lives in them. This means furthermore, that in their own lives, they are called to recapitulate the self-giving pattern embodied in Jesus's life" (Hays 2008, 346).

Michael Gorman observes, "Being in Christ both includes and transcends the local community; those who are in Christ in Corinth (like Paul) and in Rome are in Christ *together*. 'In' language is a spatial idiom that signifies a relational reality that is both personal and corporate, both 'vertical' and 'horizontal,' both local and universal" (Gorman 2019, 5). It is individual union with Christ, and it is corporate—not just the local church but various churches; it is universal.

I invite you now to go back and read over the above list of verses with Gorman's and Hays's observations in mind. What do you feel? What comes to mind now when you read these phrases of union with Christ? What stands out to you? What changes in your reading?

We have worked to understand what Paul means when he says "in Christ" or "united with Christ." It is an important task because as we observed, it is a theme much more common in Paul than "justification by faith." It matters what we see as foundational and central in Paul. If we see union with Christ—in its broad, deep, and corporate way—as foundational in Paul's writings how will that shape the way we think of the atonement? Salvation? Discipleship?

—

United with Christ in death and life (2:19-21). It is difficult to know what Paul meant by the phrase, "through the law I died to the law" (2:19). It could mean through following the law religiously he came to experience that it dealt death rather than life. Or, if we read it in relation to the next verse and his union with Christ on the cross, he could be communicating that people enslaved to religious distortion of the law crucified Jesus and through that crucifixion Paul was liberated from his religious zealotry to live for God. Although we cannot be sure about the first part of the verse, the latter part is clear, he is living for God. Think of what a contrast this is to the Paul of the past. Rather than saying "I died to the law," he would have said something like, "I am willing to die for the law," and probably even, "I am willing to kill to defend the law."

In verse 20, Paul is not referring to a unique, private, mystical experience. As we have seen above, for Paul union with Christ's death is true of all who are in Christ. We can see an expanded description of "crucified with Christ" in Paul's letter to the Romans.

> Or don't you know that all of us who were baptized into Christ Jesus were baptized into his death? We were therefore buried with him through baptism into death in order that, just as Christ was raised from the dead through the glory of the Father, we too may live a new life.

> For if we have been united with him in a death like his, we will certainly also be united with him in a resurrection like his. For we know that our old self was *crucified with him* so that the body ruled by sin might be done away with, that we should no longer

be slaves to sin— because anyone who has died has
been set free from sin (Romans 6:3-7, italics added).

We once again face the same translation question as in verse 16.
Does Paul live by faith in the Son of God or by the faithfulness of
the Son of God? I think the latter option is better. As Richard Hays
states, "Paul is not claiming that he lives now by 'believing in' the
Son of God; he has, in fact just (rhetorically) denied any continuing
personal agency at all. Instead, it is now the [faithfulness] of the
Son of God, Jesus Christ's own self-giving faithfulness, that moves
in and through him. The life that he now lives 'in the flesh' (i.e. in
embodied historical existence) is both animated and determined
by Jesus Christ's faithfulness" (Hays 2000, 244).

The "faithfulness of" translation puts the emphasis on God's
action—like the latter part of the verse ("who loved me and gave
himself for me"). As Michael Gorman points out it also underscores
it is not just the cross, the crucifixion event, but the Spirit of the
Crucified one that liberates and empowers. Gorman offers this
paraphrase of 2:19-20: "It is no longer I or we who live our own
lives, but it is God's crucified and resurrected Messiah who lives
in me and in us by his Spirit, empowering us to embody his kind
of faithfulness and love" (Gorman 2013, 67).

The Greek root of the word "righteousness" in 2:21 is the same
as "justified" in 2:16. In fact some translations render this verse as,
"if justification comes through the law." Thus in this final verse
he returns to the central issue of who can join together in table
fellowship. If people could be brought into right relationship with
God and others, joined together regardless of ethnicity, through
works of the law, then, Paul argues, Christ death was not necessary.
That is not the case. It is through the cross that God has worked
to make things right, to liberate from the present evil age and

its religious and ethnic bounded systems of distinction. As we observed in chapter 3, Paul proclaims that God has graciously acted not just toward those of worthy status, but toward all. Paul has not set aside this grace. Rather it is Peter, the Jerusalem party, and the agitators in Galatia, and their bounded group religiosity that nullifies God's grace. When Peter gave priority to boundary lines based on circumcision and dietary laws and pulled away from the united table at Antioch he was living as if the cross were of no effect. Those that are crucified with Christ do not draw lines of exclusion but eat together at the same table.

Implications of the Text for Today

Give more attention to Paul's "in Christ" theme. Many of us have a feeble understanding of union with Christ and overlook its centrality in Paul's letters. Let us look for ways to strengthen our corporate-thinking muscles. Perhaps a start is to underline this language when we encounter it in Paul; and, when we do so pause and, with examples from contemporary life of union in mind, reflect on a more collective participatory reading of that verse.

Broad Understanding of Centered on Jesus Christ. I frequently state that to say Jesus Christ is our center is not just to have beliefs about Jesus as our center. The person Jesus Christ is our center. The Pauline "in Christ" theme broadens even further the meaning and import of centering on Jesus. To have Christ as center includes the experience of participation in Christ, of living and dying with Jesus Christ. That shapes our walk individually and corporately.

We are in Christ together with others. Many of us already feel a sense of kinship with other Christians—locally and around the world. Placing more emphasis on *my* being united with Christ calls for an even more heightened sense of union with *others* united with Christ.

Individual encounter with Jesus is important. Although I have argued that concern for the health and unity of the Galatian church communities fueled Paul's passion in this letter, that does not mean individuals and their relationship with God did not concern him. In the previous chapter we observed how the religious actions of Peter and those from Jerusalem divided the community and also likely impacted individuals and their relationship with God. In this chapter we have observed that in the final part of the section on Antioch, Paul writes of his individual experience. This underscores that it is not either community or individual, but both. Note, however, that the individual experience with Jesus that Paul describes here includes much more than simply release from guilt. To be crucified with Christ produces a radical life change including, in this case, leaving behind the practice of bounded group religiosity and the embrace of people previously viewed as unworthy, "contaminated," or even the enemy. Let us proclaim the gospel to individuals, but let it be the deep and radical gospel we see in this letter.

Personal Response

- From the first pages of this book I have argued that we miss the depth and richness of this letter if we think the central issue was seeking to correct a teaching that salvation is by works. That does not mean, however, that grace and works are not important themes in the letter. Paul mentions them explicitly in the last verse in this section. It is not that the common reading of Galatians being about grace and works is wrong. Rather, it is too narrow and superficial. Based on your reading of the letter up to this point, how has your understanding of grace and works changed? How has it broadened and deepened?

- I invite you to re-read Richard Hays's and Michael Gorman's comments on verses 19-20. Try to visualize what they write. How have you experienced this in your life? How might it shape your life today, this week?

- If you did not do so, take time to reflect on the questions at the end of the "In Christ" section.

- We have been in chapter two for an extended period. Before starting the next chapter you may want to re-read through the whole letter to reflect on how Galatians 2 relates to the whole, and to have the full letter freshly in mind as we begin exploring Galatians 3.

CHAPTER SEVEN

Contrasting Identities

The Text: Galatians 3:1-14

3 You foolish Galatians! Who has bewitched you? Before your very eyes Jesus Christ was clearly portrayed as crucified. 2 I would like to learn just one thing from you: Did you receive the Spirit by the works of the law, or by believing what you heard? 3 Are you so foolish? After beginning by means of the Spirit, are you now trying to finish by means of the flesh? 4 Have you experienced so much in vain—if it really was in vain? 5 So again I ask, does God give you his Spirit and work miracles among you by the works of the law, or by your believing what you heard? 6 So also Abraham "believed God, and it was credited to him as righteousness."

7 Understand, then, that those who have faith are children of Abraham. 8 Scripture foresaw that God would justify the Gentiles by faith, and announced the gospel in advance to Abraham: "All nations will be blessed through you." 9 So those who rely on faith are blessed along with Abraham, the man of faith.

[10] *For all who rely on the works of the law are under a curse, as it is written: "Cursed is everyone who does not continue to do everything written in the Book of the Law." [11] Clearly no one who relies on the law is justified before God, because "the righteous will live by faith." [12] The law is not based on faith; on the contrary, it says, "The person who does these things will live by them." [13] Christ redeemed us from the curse of the law by becoming a curse for us, for it is written: "Cursed is everyone who is hung on a pole." [14] He redeemed us in order that the blessing given to Abraham might come to the Gentiles through Christ Jesus, so that by faith we might receive the promise of the Spirit.*

The Flow and Form of the Text

Up to this point much of the letter has had a narrative quality, beginning autobiographically and then informing the Galatians about events and discussions in Jerusalem and Antioch. Paul now shifts from narrative and turns to address the Galatians directly as he did in the beginning of the letter. Starting here and continuing to 5:1, Paul offers a series of arguments responding to what the other missionaries have likely said to the Galatians.

Paul begins with an argument rooted in their experience and then in verse six he turns to base his argument in scripture. Apparently the agitators have communicated through their words and bounded group actions that the Galatian Christians cannot truly be daughters and sons of Abraham without practicing the works of the law that distinguish Jews from others. Paul will use scripture to show that is not the case (3:6-9; 26-29). Since the other missionaries have spoken so positively of the law, Paul needs to address the obvious question of his perspective on the law (3:10-25).

The Text Explained

Works of the law vs. the Spirit has worked (3:1-5). What strong words! It is as if Paul shouts out, "Foolish Galatians!" and then he likens the agitators to witches who have cast a spell over them. It is likely that remembering the tragic division of the church community in Antioch has re-kindled the passion we saw earlier in 1:6. He does not want the same thing to occur in the Galatian churches. His deeply felt words remind us again that although doctrinal themes are present in this letter, it was not a scholarly debate between theologians over intricacies of doctrine. Paul, a missionary theologian, was compelled to write the letter by concrete situations that deeply concerned him, including: enslavement to religion, failure to live out the truth of the gospel, and threats to the unity of the community.

Although 3:1 marks the clear start of a new section of the letter, themes from the previous section are woven into the new material. Paul continues with the same logic of the previous verses and portrays the cross of Christ in clear conflict with what the agitators are saying and doing. Similarly to what he said to Peter, it is as if Paul is asking them, "How can it be that you have forgotten the cross and are living as if Christ's death had not already included you within the people of God?" He had questioned Peter about "works of the law"—actions like circumcision and dietary rules that the agitators used to draw boundary lines. Now he questions the Galatians on "works of the law." He begins by saying, "I would like to learn just one thing from you" (3:2). It is as if Paul is saying, "This will clinch it, answer this and the argument will be over."

Through Paul's rhetorical questions he communicates, again, that they do not need to take up the Jewish customs suggested by the other missionaries in order to be worthy of God's grace or to truly belong to God's people. They have already experienced the reality of the Spirit and God has worked miracles without them complying with the "works of the law." God's actions were not conditional on them being circumcised or living like Jews. Circumcision did not produce miracles; God did. Paul points to the ridiculousness of starting with the Spirit and then going back to the flesh—a word with double meaning in this setting as both human effort and the flesh of circumcision. Paul proclaims, "You are already 'in,' God is at work. Why now worry about entrance requirements?" Peter used a similar argument in Acts 10. While Peter preached in Cornelius' house, to the astonishment of the circumcised Jewish believers, the Spirit descended on the Gentiles gathered there (10:44). Peter then said, "Surely no one can stand in the way of their being baptized with water. They have received the Holy Spirit just as we have" (10:47). Although the bounded group mentality of the agitators led them to disagree, Paul points to the truth that the Galatians needed no other validation than that they were part of the community of Jesus-followers.

Source of identity (3:6-12). Before exploring Paul's words about Abraham, it is helpful to reflect on some of the reasons the other missionaries' emphasis on living like Jews might have felt attractive to the Galatians. In an environment where religion played an important role in life, Christian Gentiles did not have a clear religious identity. When they turned to Jesus they would have stopped going to local temples and participating in religious rituals with others in their cities. They also, however, were not seen as part of the Jewish community—by Jews or others. They gathered in homes, rather than temples or synagogues, and did not belong to a known and accepted religion. In an individualistic society, standing outside the norm in this way might not cause much personal turmoil, but they lived in an honor-shame society where what others thought of one's group was of immense importance. The other missionaries' comments and bounded group attitudes likely caused the Gentile Christians to doubt even their identity as Christians and led them to feel more shame and insecurity. At the same time the other missionaries held out the promise of an identity more accepted in the Galatian context. They could have the security of being seen as belonging to the Jewish religion—true sons and daughters of Abraham. It is understandable that the Galatians felt attracted to this option, and notable that Paul does not ignore their sense of insecurity. Although he argues against their taking the step of living like Jews, he accepts the importance of identity and of feeling part of a group. His response, however, is to reaffirm that they already are part of Abraham's family.

We see the trajectory of Paul's argument in 3:6-9 in the first three words, "So also Abraham." Paul equates Abraham's experience with that of the Galatians (3:2-5). Like theirs, Abraham's experience is rooted in God's grace, not in "works of the law." Paul makes the point through quoting Genesis 15:6, Abraham "believed God, and it was credited to him as righteousness." It is not just the words that are important, but also their place in the chronology of Abraham's story. The agitators very likely emphasized Genesis 17, when Abraham obeyed God's command of circumcision, as evidence of the necessity of circumcision for those who want to belong to the family of Abraham. Paul points out that Abraham was justified *before* he was circumcised and thus the foundation in the history of Abraham is not circumcision, but God's promise and Abraham's trust in that promise.

Paul then takes the next logical step:, those who trust in God as Abraham did are children of Abraham (3:7, 9). Once again, digging a bit deeper into translation of the Greek opens up the meaning to us. The NIV opts for "those who have faith are children of Abraham." A more literal translation, as seen in NASB and KJV, is, "those who are of faith are children of Abraham." It is a bit awkward, and we can understand why other translations opt for wording that flows easier. Yet the more literal translation illuminates two things. First, it includes a sense of group identity. J. Louis Martyn offers a translation that captures this well: "those whose identity is derived from faith" (Martyn 1997, 294). Second, the literal translation enables us to see the parallel with the same Greek structure in 2:12, "those who were of the circumcision" (KJV), and 3:10, "who are of the works of the law" (NASB, KJV). Martyn's parallel translation of 3:10 is "Those whose identity is derived from observance of the Law" (Martyn 1997, 307).

Let us look at Paul's phrases through the lens of bounded, fuzzy, and centered sets. Those who build their identity on circumcision, sabbath observance, and dietary laws are a bounded group. They use those works of a law to draw a line that distinguishes those who are in the group and those who are not. It is noteworthy that Paul does not take a bounded approach. He does not debate with the works-of-the-law group about the correct content of the boundary line. He does not, for instance, set up a those-who-are-of-Jesus'-commands group. Neither does he simply erase the lines and take a fuzzy approach. The group of those who are of the faith are distinct from other people. He does not say, "there is no distinction, everyone is in God's family." He offers a third option, a fully different paradigm. He erases boundary lines, but still gives the Galatians a strong sense of identity rooted in their relationship with the center—Jesus Christ. Their faith, and their gaze, is on God's gracious action. It is that orientation toward the center, not a boundary line, that provides distinction from others.

In the next step in his argument (3:8-9), Paul again uses Genesis (12:3; 18:18; 22:18) to demonstrate that the inclusion of non-Jews in the family of Abraham is not a new idea but was found in early promises to Abraham by God. Then Paul takes up the question of the law.

Significant Concept: Law

Not only in these verses (3:10-14), but throughout this letter Paul speaks negatively of the law. What is the problem of the law? The curse of the law? Many would say that the problem Paul points to is seeking salvation through keeping the law, falling short and therefore being cursed—experiencing the wrath of God. Hans Boersma points out three errors in this common interpretation of Paul and the law (Boersma 2004, 173-74). First, this interpretation errs by ignoring social and historical context—both of Galatia and of Israel in the Old Testament. Second, it is an erroneous understanding that in the Old Testament salvation was by works and in the New Testament it is by grace. Also, as explained in chapter two, and in the section on Grace in chapter three, the agitators did not think this way or teach salvation by works. If Paul had presented this as the problem with the law, the other missionaries could have easily dismissed his argument. They would say they did not claim to have kept all the law without fail and would point out that within the law itself God provided means for forgiveness of sins and transgression of the law through repentance, sacrifices, and the Day of Atonement (Leviticus 23:26-32). Finally, Boersma observes that when we read Paul's comments on the law we should think of communities, not just individuals.

If the curse of the law was not having to avoid transgression in order to be saved, what did Paul consider the curse of the law?

We begin with an affirmation that appears to contradict what Paul writes in Galatians. The law given by God to Israel in the Old Testament was good, an instrument of life and *shalom*. Paul himself makes this affirmation elsewhere. In his letter to the Romans he states that the law was intended to bring life. "The law is holy, and the commandment is holy, righteous and good" (Romans 7:10, 12). He makes a number of other positive statements about the law (Romans 3:31; 9:4; 13:8-10; I Corinthians 7:19). Yet in his letter to Galatians Paul writes negatively about the law. Rather than nuancing and bending his various statements to try to make them not sound contradictory, it is best to recognize Paul is talking about different things. In the positive statements he is talking about the law as given by God, in the negative ones he is talking about the law taken up by the power religion which twists it into a negative force. (For more on relating religion to Pauline principality and power language, see chapter two.)

This is an example of the importance of remembering that Paul is a missionary theologian writing letters focused on specific issues. His "books" in the New Testament are not an ongoing project in systematic theology. Rather than demanding the coherence we would expect in the latter, let us expect him to adjust his language to the situation—as we do. (For instance, in this book I use the term "religion" in a negative way, but there are other contexts in which I use the term at least neutrally if not positively. That is not because of some internal debate but because I adapt to the way the term is used and understood for the audience.) Rather than approach Paul's negative use of the term "law" in Galatians in contrast to statements elsewhere as a problem to be solved, let us put our energy into understanding how he is using the term in this letter.

Although Paul has referred positively to Abraham and Jewish scriptures, up to this point in the letter he has always spoken negatively of Judaism, Jewish traditions, and the works of the law, describing them in ways that match what I call bounded group religiosity. Therefore, in the literary context of this letter and the concrete context of the churches of Galatia it makes sense that Paul would talk of the law as an instrument of religion.

In a centered group the law helps people come closer to God and live in harmony with others. As a community under the influence of religion moves toward becoming a bounded group they switch their identity from their relationship with the God of the center to their standing with the boundary line. The law, or "works of the law," came to function as this boundary line. This occurred at various times in the Old Testament, in the Judaism that Paul practiced, and the Christianity of the other missionaries. Shifting identity to the boundary line and the law distorted their concept of God and their understanding of how the law functioned in a context of grace. They had failed and were cursed, but not because of particular sinful actions, or because they could not obey all the law. They failed because they misinterpreted the relation between the law and their identity as the people of God.

Therefore, when we read Paul make negative comments about the law in this letter we do well to think of it as closely aligned with bounded group religiosity—law as an instrument of religion, not as a gracious gift from God.

—

What Paul writes here (3:10-14) is closely connected to what we observed in the conflict at Antioch and his words about justification, inclusion in the family of God, in Galatians 2:16. There Paul stated that one is not justified or included based on "works of the law." Here he describes what happens with those who try to be justified through practices that distinguish Jews from others. As we have already observed, in contrast to those whose identity is derived from faith (3:9), Paul now writes of those whose identity is derived from observance of the law (3:10). It is easy to imagine that his words must have left listeners stunned. He says the exact opposite of the agitators. Those they would have said are blessed, those of the "works of the law," Paul calls cursed, and he calls the Gentile Christians, those of the faith, blessed.

As you read Paul's quotes from the Old Testament, keep in mind the context. He is talking about those whose identity is in the "works of the law." It is as if he is saying, "Be careful, once you shift your identity from a shared trust in God to a shared compliance with a boundary line you then will have to always work to maintain your membership status through staying on the right side of the line." The security offered by the clear boundary line may attract them, but in a bounded group approach they will live under the constant threat of shameful exclusion if they fail to meet the standards. To live by the law in a bounded religious way impacts individuals and changes the character of the group.

The cross and the curse of the law (3:13-14). In 3:13 Paul again quotes words from scripture, this time to make a connection between Jesus, the cross, and the curse of the law. He uses words related to atonement theology (how the cross provides salvation), words like "redemption" and "for us" (substitution). Familiarity with these themes can lead to two errors. One would be to make little comment on the verse, thinking we know what this is about, it is clear enough. A second would be to give a full and detailed explanation based on a particular theory of atonement. That would be like taking a chapter out of a systematic theology book and inserting it here without giving attention to the context of this verse. I will take a middle path, not just repeating the words of the verse, but also not pretending to give a complete explanation of how Jesus' death and resurrection provide salvation. The depth of God's work through the cross cannot be communicated in one verse. Seeking to interpret the verse in its context, we will read the verse through the lens of enslaving religion and the curse of a bounded group that excludes and shames.

Jesus confronted, through his words and actions, bounded group religiosity and the status system of his day. He erased lines of division and tore down walls of exclusion when he showered acceptance and honor on shamed outsiders. He warned insiders of the curse of their religiosity. Religion as a power, its institutional instruments and humans in its grip, reacted aggressively against Jesus with an increasing hostility that culminated in the crucifixion. It was the ultimate move of shaming and exclusion. In his life Jesus was cursed for standing with the excluded and in his death he suffered the worst of the curse of bounded group religiosity. He suffered that shame and exclusion in the place of others—both the excluders and the excluded, the shamers and the shamed. But religion and its violent curse did not have the final word. Through the resurrection of Jesus, God exposed and disarmed this power (see also, Galatians 1:4, 5:1 and Colossians 2:15).

In the next verse (14), Paul communicates the result of the work of the cross he proclaimed in verse 13. It has universal significance; the Galatian Christians are included. I invite you, however, to pause, read this verse and think of Paul. Through the cross of Jesus, Paul experienced a radical transformation. Think back over this section of Galatians, where he is arguing against positions he previously held. Imagine what the pre-encounter-with-Jesus Paul would have thought about his comments here about the law! His conversion was not an encounter with new information that changed a doctrinal perspective. It was not that he previously thought one was saved by works and now he recognizes salvation is by grace. Rather his encounter with the crucified and risen Christ went way beyond changing a point of doctrine; it was a profound paradigm change, a new way of seeing. Richard Hays calls it a conversion of the imagination.

Hays explains that Paul did not promote a Christian Judaism like the Judaism of his past except for now including Gentiles. Rather, the "Israel" that the Galatian converts were brought into was an Israel whose history and identity had been radically reinterpreted and reconfigured by the cross and resurrection. "The result was that Jew and Gentile alike found themselves summoned by the gospel story to a sweeping re-evaluation of their identities, an imaginative paradigm shift so comprehensive that it can only be described as a 'conversion of the imagination'" (Hays 1999, 395). In terms of this commentary we could say that previously Paul could only imagine bounded group approaches. He could see no other way of establishing his identity and living as a faithful Jew.

I love Hays's phrase and use it when I teach Galatians. It both underscores how radically different a centered approach is, and it also underscores that to change from a bounded to centered way is no small thing. It requires not just explanations describing the paradigm, but a conversion of the imagination. Yet a friend who was correcting the Spanish on my handouts suggested I not use the phrase when teaching in Latin America. He feared people in my classes or seminars would not get it—they would think I was talking about "imaginary." With that in mind, when teaching a course on Galatians in Colombia I took time to explain the phrase. Just that week a peace accord had been signed after 52 years of war. I said, "Most of you in this room have never lived in a Colombia not at war. You need a new way of thinking about your country. You need a conversion of the imagination, and it requires imagination because you do not know a Colombia not at war." At the end of the course, one of the students, displaced by the war, said the most impactful thing for her from the course was the phrase "conversion of the imagination." It summed up the course for her.

For Paul, and for us, the conversion of the imagination from bounded to centered comes through encounter with Jesus. Paul had been totally committed to guard the boundary lines that he thought identified his people as the family of God. Now he is totally dedicated to preaching a gospel centered on Jesus that breaks down the walls of division and includes Gentiles. The work of the cross produced concrete transformation that led to the blessing of the nations promised to Abraham.

Implications of the Text for Today

God communicates truth through various means. In the first chapter Paul emphasized truth received by revelation from God. In 2:10-14 he presented unity in Christ, the act of eating together, as an expression of the truth of the gospel. In his comments to Peter (2:10-21) he presented information, or we could say doctrine, as an aspect of truth. In the section studied in this chapter he included Old Testament history and quotes from scripture as elements of truth and appealed to their experience of God's Spirit as evidence of truth. Let us not have a narrow concept of truth but recognize with Paul that God communicates truth through a combination of means: Scripture, experience of God in our lives, theology written by others throughout church history, and truth lived out with others.

Value in emphasizing what Paul did not say about the law. I listed interpretive mistakes that lead people to the erroneous view that Paul's purpose is to point out that it is impossible to obey all the law and those who try to do so will be cursed by their failure. I would now like to list some of the problematic fruit of that mistaken interpretation. First, those who believe that salvation is by grace, not by obeying all of the law, will see this text as for others—those who think they can earn their salvation. In contrast, the interpretation offered in this chapter opens the significance of the text for all. We are all at risk of falling under the sway of religion and twisting a faith rooted in grace into bounded group religiosity as some Jews did with the law. Second, to think that Paul's point is to say it is impossible to obey all the law can lead to viewing the Old Testament as a plan that did not work. It leads to thinking that salvation by obeying the law did not work, so God went to plan B—grace and Jesus. Or, less extreme, but still not adequate, it can lead to thinking the purpose of the law was to make us all aware that we fall short, that we cannot earn our salvation by good works. Although it is true we are sinners, the law does much more than reveal that. Both of these perspectives can lead people to seeing little purpose in reading the law specifically and the Old Testament in general. That is a great loss, especially in a time of concern over environmental degradation, increasing inequality, mistreatment of immigrants, and ever-present issues of poverty and injustice. The Old Testament has much to offer on these themes. Therefore, let us correct erroneous thinking about the law and present it as a gift given by a loving God.

Freedom from the curse of bounded group religiosity. Correcting mistaken interpretations is important, but we must not stop there. This passage has positive implications. It not only presents the reality of the curse of religion, but also communicates to us that through Christ we can live free of that curse. It points to the divisiveness and exclusion that flow from rooting our identity in the lines drawn by a bounded group, it also proclaims the possibility of rooting our identity elsewhere—in Jesus Christ.

Ongoing process. Commenting on "conversion of the imagination" and Paul's letters, Richard Hays states, "Such a thoroughgoing conversion could be fostered and sustained only by a continuous process of bringing the community's beliefs and practices into critical confrontation with the gospel story" (Hays 1999, 395). His observation points to three important implications for us seeking to live as a centered-set church today. First, the words "continuous process" communicate that freedom from bounded group religiosity is not a single step but an ongoing journey. Second, in a related way, a single hearing of the gospel story is not sufficient. We must continually return to and immerse ourselves in the radical, anti-religious, gospel of Jesus Christ. Third, "critical confrontation" points to the reality that in an ongoing way we should expect to see beliefs and practices from our bounded or fuzzy past continue to appear. It is much better to be vigilant rather than assuming we are beyond them.

Personal Response

- Paul contrasts bounded groups, whose identity is derived from circumcision and the works of the law, with the centered group, whose identity is derived from faith. If Paul was going to write a letter to your context today what are some bounded groups he would list? What are different ways he would complete this phrase: their identity is derived from _____?

- What are ways you have felt the pull of religion to turn the way of Jesus into bounded group religiosity?

- What stood out to you from looking at the cross through the lens of bounded group religiosity (both as the cross being bounded religions' reaction to Jesus and Jesus' response to bounded group religiosity)? Take some time to reflect on the significance of the cross, interpreted in this way, for your life. Try to visualize its import for your life today.

- How do you think you individually and your community of faith can increase a centered-group identity in Jesus and decrease bounded group identity?

CHAPTER EIGHT

One Family in Christ

The Text: Galatians 3:15-29

[15] *Brothers and sisters, let me take an example from everyday life. Just as no one can set aside or add to a human covenant that has been duly established, so it is in this case.* [16] *The promises were spoken to Abraham and to his seed. Scripture does not say "and to seeds," meaning many people, but "and to your seed," meaning one person, who is Christ.* [17] *What I mean is this: The law, introduced 430 years later, does not set aside the covenant previously established by God and thus do away with the promise.* [18] *For if the inheritance depends on the law, then it no longer depends on the promise; but God in his grace gave it to Abraham through a promise.*

[19] *Why, then, was the law given at all? It was added because of transgressions until the Seed to whom the promise referred had come. The law was given through angels and entrusted to a mediator.* [20] *A mediator, however, implies more than one party; but God is one.*

²¹ *Is the law, therefore, opposed to the promises of God? Absolutely not! For if a law had been given that could impart life, then righteousness would certainly have come by the law.* ²² *But Scripture has locked up everything under the control of sin, so that what was promised, being given through the faithfulness of Jesus Christ,*ᵃ *might be given to those who believe.*

²³ *Before the coming of this faith, we were held in custody under the law, locked up until the faith that was to come would be revealed.* ²⁴ *So the law was our guardian until Christ came that we might be justified by faith.* ²⁵ *Now that this faith has come, we are no longer under a guardian.*

²⁶ *So in Christ Jesus you are all children of God through faith,* ²⁷ *for all of you who were baptized into Christ have clothed yourselves with Christ.* ²⁸ *There is neither Jew nor Gentile, neither slave nor free, nor is there male and female, for you are all one in Christ Jesus.* ²⁹ *If you belong to Christ, then you are Abraham's seed, and heirs according to the promise.*

---

a. The NIV translation of 3:22 is "through faith in Jesus Christ," but "through the faithfulness of Jesus" is offered as an alternative in the footnotes. I have inserted this alternative in the text above. See further explanation in the chapter five discussion of 2:16.

The Flow and Form of the Text

In contrast to the strong words of 3:1 that are probably still ringing in their ears ("You foolish Galatians!"), Paul begins this section warmly with "brothers and sisters." He does more, however, than just communicate affection. Calling them siblings reinforces a central point in this chapter—Paul and the Galatian Christians are part of the same family, the family of God. Paul continues to mine the story of Abraham and the text of Genesis to affirm that the Gentiles' membership in that family is not a new idea. Paul also continues to contrast the law with the unity enabled by the faithfulness of Jesus Christ, culminating in Paul's ringing declaration, "There is neither Jew nor Gentile, neither slave nor free, nor is there male and female, for you are all one in Christ Jesus" (3:28). Let us explore how he builds to that statement.

The Text Explained

One family, as promised to Abraham, in and through Jesus Christ (3:15-25). To better understand the example Paul uses from everyday life (3:15), N. T. Wright invites us to picture a situation where someone has died without leaving a will or directions for their funeral. It can cause not just discussion, but heated arguments. One family member might say, "He would have liked. . ." and another counter, "No, he wanted. . . ." If the deceased left written instructions, however, it does not matter what opinions others have. Their opinions do not change what is clearly stated in the will (Wright 2004, 35–36). In a similar way, in this section Paul communicates that God's desires were made clear in the covenant with Abraham. Opinions offered later, like those of the other missionaries for instance, do not change what is already in the covenant stated in scripture.

It could appear that in verse 16 Paul makes a weak exegetical argument based on faulty grammar. He argues that the texts in Genesis do not say "seeds" (Genesis 12:7; 13:15; 17-7-10; 24:7). That is true, but in Genesis "seed" is clearly a collective noun that refers to Abraham's many descendants. It is not singular in the way Paul appears to be using the word. If we look only at the words it does appear Paul is twisting them to say something they do not in the original. Let us, however, take a step back and look at themes of the whole section. Paul is making an argument about family and who belongs. N. T. Wright, therefore, argues "that the 'singular seed' means the single family, incorporated into the Messiah" (Wright 2004, 36). This reading of "seed" in verse 16 is supported by Paul's use of the same word, "seed" in verse 29 where it is a collective noun referring to Abraham's one family. With that in mind Wright argues that, "the singularity of seed in verse 16 is not the singularity of an individual person contrasted with the plurality of many human beings, but the singularity of one family contrasted with the plurality of families which would result if Torah were to be regarded the way Paul's opponents apparently regard it" (Wright 1992, 163). Wright translates the verse in this way, "Well, the promises were made 'to Abraham and his family.' It doesn't say 'his families,' as though referring to several, but indicates one: 'and to your family'—which means the Messiah" (Wright 2004, 35).

According to Wright's translation, the divided table fellowship at Antioch is a concrete image of what Paul has in mind. The one family gathered around the table split and became two. Wright states, "If ethnic origin, racial and geographical loyalties, and the like, are to be allowed to remain as the key factors in deciding who one is allowed to eat with, that is, in determining the boundaries of the people of God, then there will be far more than two 'families.'" In relation to relating the seed with Christ, Wright invites us to keep the "in Christ" theme in mind. The seed, the one family, spoken of in the promises is, as Paul will show, the one family created in Christ (see 3:26-29). "Christ is the 'seed' because, and insofar as, the promised single family of Abraham is brought into being in and through him and him alone. It therefore finds its identity in him. He is its incorporation" (Wright 1992, 164–66). In contrast, the bounded group expression of the law that divides the Jewish Christians and Gentiles Christians into different families goes against God's covenant promise to Abraham.

If verse 16 is complicated to interpret, verses 17 and 18 are the opposite. They are easy to understand; their significance is profound. Related to the covenant example in verse 15 Paul makes the point that the law did not replace or set aside the covenant. Since the law was not given as a pre-condition to the covenant, it does not make sense for the agitators to use the law as a pre-condition for the Gentile Christians to become part of God's family. Paul says, "You're already heirs!" The chronological order sets up the point Paul makes in verse 18. God's grace is the foundation for all. The covenant promise and the inheritance are gracious acts of God. Keeping the law did not make the Jewish people worthy of God's grace. The law came after they had already experienced God's grace. Therefore, for the Galatians as well, it is not "works of the law" that make them worthy or provide their identity; it is the grace of God that makes them part of the family of God. Their identity is rooted in God's grace not in actions that place them on the right side of a boundary line drawn by humans.

After having said so many negative things about the law, and stating what it does not do, Paul turns to the obvious question, "Why, then, was the law given at all?" His answer, "because of transgressions" (3:19), is brief and direct but not clear. There are at least five different ways of interpreting the phrase. Perhaps the best two are: God gave the law to identify humanity's sinfulness as conscious transgression, or God gave the law to restrain transgression. We can see both in Galatians. Paul then continues with the theme of "seed" and one family. While other missionaries have emphasized the law of Moses, Paul states that Moses and the angels were mediators (see Deuteronomy 33:2; Acts 7:53; Hebrews 2:2). In contrast, God's covenant with Abraham was direct, without a mediator. Moses and the law did not produce the one family in the past and will not in the present.

In verse 21 Paul states emphatically that the law is not in conflict with the promises of God. It was not given as a condition for the promise, and it alone could not produce justice/righteousness. (In the New Testament the same Greek word is at times translated as "justice" and at times as "righteousness. Therefore, when either English word is used we should keep in mind the Hebraic understanding of justice described in chapter five of this book.) It is likely that in verse 22 Paul means to communicate something similar to what he writes in Romans 3:9-20. It is not that Scripture is the cause of sin, but it reveals the reality that all are under the power of sin.

He then speaks of the law as a guardian (3:23-25). In Paul's time the *paidagōgos* (literally 'child-leader') was a slave in the Greco-Roman household who supervised and guarded children. His responsibility was to walk them to and from school, to see that they behaved properly and stayed out of harm's way. The *paidagōgos*, however, was not a member of the family, and when the child grew to a certain age, his services were no longer required" (Hays 2000, 269). Paul uses this metaphor to communicate that the law had a similar role in guarding, guiding, and disciplining God's people. And like the *paidagōgos* the law was only for a certain time period until the faith would be revealed/until Christ came.

Paul returns to the theme of 2:16 and again proclaims that the promised justification—being brought into right relationship as the one family of God—is possible through the faithfulness of Jesus Christ for all those who believe (3:22). It is grace given, not achieved.

What does it mean, in verse 23, for the faith to be revealed? Here, and in the verses that follow, we see the value and importance of opting for the "faithfulness of Jesus Christ" translation in the previous verse. It continues the letter's practice of emphasizing God's action over human action; it matches both the logic of the letter and the following verses (revelation in this letter has been linked to God, not human action, and it makes more sense to talk of Christ's faithfulness being revealed, than the revelation of human faith in Christ); and it enables us to see the parallelism in the verses.

3:22	through the faithfulness of Jesus Christ
3:23	Before the coming of this faith (faithfulness)
3:23	until the faith (faithfulness) that was to come would be revealed
3:24	until Christ came that we might be justified by faith (faithfulness).
3:25	Now that this faith (faithfulness) has come

In these verses Paul uses the coming of Christ and the coming of faith/faithfulness interchangeably which points to the interwovenness of the two. Through this language Paul is likely referring again to Jesus Christ's faithful death for our sake. Inclusion in the family of God is made possible by the faithfulness of Jesus Christ. Those who believe/trust in Jesus as the means of justification root their identity in Jesus and not in a "membership card" gained through complying with religious acts of distinction.

One in Christ (3:26-29). Paul builds on and weaves together themes from the rest of the chapter: family, identity, and union with Christ. The family language is rich, "children of God" (26), "Abraham's seed" and "heirs" (3:29); and now Paul connects it explicitly to the Galatians, *"you* are all children of God" and *"you* are Abraham's seed." Paul honors them by including them in a phrase that before Paul encountered Jesus Christ he would have used to refer only to Jews. In these verses he makes clear that it is in and through Christ that they are part of the family of God: "in Christ," "into Christ," "clothed with Christ," "one in Christ Jesus," and "belong to Christ" (3:26-29).

Note that Paul does not just say you are children of God, but you *all* are children of God. And, he does not just say "all" once, but three times. It is the opposite of what the bounded group actions of the visitors communicated to Gentile Christians in Antioch. Paul's use of "all" also contrasts with the words and actions of the agitators which communicated that some of the Galatian believers were not fully part of God's family. Has Paul taken a fuzzy approach, "everyone is in"? No, the "all" is linked to baptism. The basis on which he can confidently state they are children of God is that they have all been baptized. So, he is not fuzzy, but you might wonder is he actually still bounded? The agitators used Jewish identity practices, "works of the law," to draw their line of judgment. Is Paul using baptism in a bounded way?

As described in the first chapter, a bounded church uses certain requirements to define who belongs to the group and who does not. A centered church observes someone's orientation toward Jesus, the center, to discern whether they belong to the group or not. I must first acknowledge that baptism is sometimes used in a bounded way, but in essence it is a centered act. The key factor in a centered group is direction—toward the center or away from the center. Baptism symbolizes a change of direction, that a person has turned and started a new life. In this verse Paul makes it abundantly clear that baptism is related with the center—"baptized into Christ" and "clothed with Christ" (3:27). The focus is not on the human action and meeting a standard, rather it is on union with Christ which includes turning, dying to an old life and entering a new life (see also 2:19-20 and Romans 6:3-11; 13:14; Ephesians 4:22-24; Colossians 3:9-10). It is probable that at that time, baptism included removing one's clothes before and putting on new clothes after the baptism to symbolize the new life of union with Christ. The baptized person's identity is not in "works of the law" or in baptism as a line-crossing requirement, their identity comes from their union with Christ, the center. This produces a community with a radically different character than a bounded group as Paul makes explicit in the following verse.

Highlighting baptism rather than circumcision is already an expression of what Paul will proclaim in the next verse. Imagine what it felt like to be a Gentile Christian woman hearing all this talk about circumcision. Although there were other "works of the law" that a woman could also practice to live like a Jew, the fact is that the act most emphasized was for men only. Galatian Gentile Christian women must have felt doubly excluded—once for not being Jewish and then for not being included in the central act that could allow them to claim status like a Jew. Paul's focusing on baptism in Christ erased both those lines of exclusion.

Paul's mention of baptism also provides additional insight to our ongoing discussion about whether his letter focuses on a concern for individuals or for communities. Each person must make a personal decision to trust Christ, to turn to the way of Christ. In that sense baptism is an individual act. Yet baptism is also a communal act. A person cannot baptize themselves. It takes place in a community; it is done by others in the community and is a commitment not just to Jesus but to his body, the church. Once again, it is not either or, but both individual and community.

"There is neither Jew nor Gentile, neither slave nor free, nor is there male and female, for you are all one in Christ Jesus" (3:28).

We can sense some of the radicalness of this verse because of importance given to status differentials today. Paul's words were even more radical in the first century. I invite you to imagine for a moment hearing this same verse in the honor-shame culture described in chapter one. In society at the time of Paul, people said the exact opposite of what he writes in verse 28. They drew sharp lines of distinction between the status of Jews and Gentiles, slaves and free, men and women. Jewish morning prayers, from about the time of Paul, included these lines, "Blessed be He that He did not make me a Gentile; blessed be He that He did not make me a slave (or ignorant peasant); blessed be He that He did not make me a woman" (Witherington 1998, 271). In this prayer we observe not just a bounded group's drawing lines of distinction, but also the attitude of status superiority by those on the right side of the lines. People in Galatia and throughout the Roman world were constantly evaluating status and seeking to gain honor.

These words stating a revolutionary realignment of the ways of the world are tethered to two poles at the beginning and end of the letter. Liberation from the present evil age enables this new creation (1:4 and 6:15). "Whereas the present age is defined by differentiation, . . . new creation is a place where the value of the evil age's binary divisions have been removed" (Harvey 2016, 163). Paul's statement in this verse is also closely related to his theological reflection about the situation in Antioch (2:11-21). If believers are included at the table of God's people by the faithful obedience of Jesus rather than by actions that distinguish Jews from Gentiles, then "There is neither Jew nor Gentile, neither slave nor free, nor is there male and female." This statement at the end of chapter three flows from what he has declared throughout the chapter. If they are in one family and their identity is rooted in Christ, then their identity is not determined by whether they are Jew or Gentile, slave or free, male or female.

That does not mean their concrete reality will change. If they are a slave, they will still be a slave, if a woman, still a woman, etc. As John Barclay observes it is not that "these social/physiological conditions cease to exist, but [that] they cease to carry the symbolic value they enjoy outside of Christ; they are relativized not by a doctrine of equality but because those baptized into Christ are constituted by a gift that disregards all traditional differentials in worth" (Barclay 2014, 308). Clothing was one marker of social position; Paul tells them they are now clothed by Christ. Paul's declaration is not a mere moderation or small adjustment; it is a radical reimagining of social perspectives and practice. Paul proclaims they are free from status measurement and freed from the shame of low status. And, implicit in the declaration is an imperative—stop grasping for honor and putting others down to raise yourself up. It is unnecessary in Christ.

David Harvey makes the important observation that although the central point of controversy in the Galatian churches was over circumcision and whether Gentile believers needed to live like Jews, Paul does not stop with the first couplet. The inclusion of the other two pairs (slave-free, male-female) points to Paul's concerns going beyond a debate about circumcision. Instead, he believes that in Christ all "social categories have had their value nullified" (Harvey 2016, 179). Therefore, any line-drawing activity that distinguishes superior from inferior, honorable from shamed, and included from excluded is against the way of Christ.

Before exploring each couplet more in depth, I want to go back to one small word in Barclay's quote—"gift." The social implications of God's grace have been largely lost for those of us who have been unaware of the distinctive radicalness of Paul's concept of grace (see essay on grace in chapter three). In society at that time differentials of worth mattered in every aspect of life—including whether someone was worthy of a gift. In a context where others understand God's grace as only given to the worthy, Paul proclaimed God's gift being available to all regardless of worth. Thus Barclay states that God's grace *constituted* a fellowship of people freed from status differentiation. God's grace was not given because of the worth of the recipients; it created the worth of the recipients (Barclay 2020, xviii). It is not just that grace provides release from guilt, or future salvation, it changes concrete realities of how people view and relate to each other. All are worthy of dignity and respect, not because of their status in society, but because they are confirmed as having worth through receiving God's gift.

Beverly Gaventa would say it is not just that we have the *possibility* of recognizing the worthiness of all and breaking down societal walls of division. It is not an option. She writes,

> As the gospel's arrival obliterates the Law, it also obliterates those other "places" with which people identify themselves, even the most fundamental places of ethnicity, economic and social standing, and gender. The only location available for those grasped by the gospel is "in Christ." In Paul's view, then, it is as impossible for the Galatians to be simultaneously "in" the world of the Law and "in" Christ as it is for them to be "in" the world of their former paganism and "in" Christ (Gaventa 2000, 272).

She argues that this is why Paul takes such an uncompromising stance with the agitators. Compromise assumes the possibility of shared territory, a possibility Paul cannot fathom.

We will explore each of the couplets, as identified by Gaventa (ethnicity, economic and social standing, and gender) and then conclude with further general comments.

Ethnicity: Paul writes "There is neither Jew nor Gentile." Yet in the present evil age (1:4), there was a great distinction between Jew and Gentile in the bounded group religiosity of the Judaism of Paul's past (1:13-14), and in the bounded group religiosity of the Christianity of the agitators and the visitors from Jerusalem (2:3-5; 12-16; 6:12). They used certain works of the law to form the line that marked a distinction between Jew and Gentile. In contrast, Paul points to Christian Jews and Christian Gentiles eating together at one table as a manifestation of the truth of the gospel (2:11-14). Together, in Christ, they constitute the new people of God. The ethnic divisions based in works of the law are not just unnecessary, they are counter to the gospel.

At times a majority ethnic or racial group will allow minority groups to integrate into their world. But they expect the outsiders to adapt and live according to the ways of the majority. The other missionaries took that approach with Gentiles joining God's family. They did not totally close the door to Gentile converts. They were open to welcoming these Gentile followers of Jesus to the family table if the males would get circumcised and if they all would live like Jews. Paul proclaims something much more radical. It is a conversion of imagination mentioned in the previous chapter. The centered way of Paul is a totally different paradigm. He is not just proposing easier entrance requirements. He proclaims new creation in and through Christ. The identity and security of the individuals and the community flows from their union with Christ and not from cultural norms.

Economic and Social Standing: Paul writes, "There is . . . neither slave nor free." Yet in first-century Rome there were slaves, perhaps up to a third of the population. Within the categories of both slaves and free people there were further categories and social stratification. There were immense economic disparities and great differences in honor and privilege between various classes within society. In contrast, followers of Jesus based their identity in being "children of God" (3:26). They addressed each other as sister and brother—regardless of the person's rank and standing in the world. Néstor O. Miguez highlights how exceptional this was in their context. "Among all the religions of antiquity . . . Christianity was the only one that used the appellative of 'brothers, sisters' with people of different ethnicities, social positions, or legal standing" (Miguez 2010, 1046).[*]

In Christ, social distinctions were eliminated. Yet, when a slave or a peasant stepped out of their fellowship they walked back into a still stratified world. As we wonder why Paul did not address that reality it is important to remember that he expected the imminent return of Christ and thought the world in its present form would soon pass away (I Cor 7:31). Richard Hays writes,

> The key to understanding Paul's thought on this question is to recognize that he sees the church as an alternative community that prefigures the new creation in the midst of a world that continues to resist God's justice. Thus Paul is not calling for a revolution in which slaves rise up and demand freedom; rather, in this verse he is declaring that God has created a new community, the church, in which the baptized already share equality (Hays 2000, 272).

Gender: Paul writes, "nor is there male and female." In contrast, in Roman society women were treated as inferior. Beverly Gaventa

---

* My translation.

clarifies that to erase the privileges and status of these categories is not to imply "sameness." For instance, elsewhere Paul writes of differing gifts (I Corinthians 12-14). She states, "Being 'in Christ' does not mean that we become part of some bland, over-cooked and underseasoned stew, in which the infinite array of women's gifts (and men's gifts) lose their particularity. Instead, it means that the first and most important thing to be said about us is that we are 'in Christ'" (Gaventa 2000, 276).

People, myself included, often quote just the powerful lines of verse 28. Yet Paul's declaration in that verse is sandwiched by important words integrally related to it. Baptism into Christ, being clothed with Christ, sets the stage and enable what he describes in verse 28. In the verse that follows he returns to a major theme of the chapter declaring to the Galatians that because they are in Christ they are part of the family of God. His words in verse 29 also point to what is the alternative. In the world it is "us" vs "them" categories, status stratification, and differing privileges. In Christ they are family and treat each other as sisters and brothers.

We gain a much greater appreciation for the shocking nature of Paul's words if we enter into a narrative that helps us feel the marked distinctions between people at that time and their strict application in daily life. As mentioned earlier, I highly recommend the following narratives written by experts on the New Testament and the ancient world: *The Lost Letters of Pergamum,* by Bruce W. Longenecker, *Going to Church in the First Century* by Robert Banks, and *A Week in the Life of Rome* by James Papandrea. They give a feel for the normal ways of the world and the radicalness of churches' fellowship. The authors paint scenes of table fellowship where rich and poor, slaves and free, Jews and Gentiles, people of high and low honor status all eat together. Their books portray how the church not only rejected the distorted concepts of honor of the society, but also replaced them with a new honor code. In the upside-down way of Jesus the churches honored those who served others rather than those who grasped for greater status and honor in society.

To conclude I want to make a few observations about God. Paul does not just say something like, "Now that we are Christians we are going to leave the bounded group religiosity, racial and class prejudice, and sexual discrimination behind. Let's use a centered approach now." Note that Christ or God is mentioned six times in these four verses. The most important words of verse 28 are not the contrasting pairs, but "in Christ Jesus." What can we learn from Paul's emphasis on God in these verses? First, it tells us something about the character of God. The God revealed by Jesus Christ stands opposed to the distorted ways that society assigns value and privilege. Second, it tells us this new reality is first and foremost about God's action not human effort to achieve what Paul declares. It is grace. Third, it reinforces what we observed in chapter 3 of this book, Paul presents God's grace as not dependent on a person's or a group's measure of worth. Finally, it displays the point that we cannot separate a bounded church paradigm or a centered church paradigm from our concept of God. If a person, or a community, view God as a judgmental figure of conditional love, they will not be able to live out what Paul proclaims in his stirring words in verse 28. That is why Paul reacts so strongly against the "gospel" of the agitators. To distort who God is and the character of God's grace will hinder a Christian community from living as family in the way Paul proclaims in these verses.

Implications of the Text for Today

Beyond equality. As noted above, in this passage Paul focuses on relationships within the church. Let us not, however, take this as license to ignore those suffering discrimination and loss of dignity in society. Other parts of scripture call us to lovingly work to liberate people from racial, economic, social, and gender-based oppression. It is a good thing to work for greater equality through more just structures. Yet, if one error would be to pay no heed to discrimination and oppression outside the church, another would be to borrow the world's standards for equality as the goal within the church. Paul presents the ideal of family—sisters and brothers in Christ.

Beverly Gaventa passionately calls us, within the church, to press much further than societally legislated efforts at equality—both because they are not enough and because, in Christ, we have the potential for more.

Our deep attachment to corrupt systems of measurement, our distorted quest for identity, to say nothing of the malformed relationships between men and women—all of these are more than attitudes in need of adjustment. They are symptoms of the persistence of the "present evil age" with which the gospel collides. No social agenda will correct the situation, and no pedagogical strategy will suffice, because the power of evil is such that it can corrupt even the purest motives and the sternest resolve (Gaventa 2000, 277–78).

Gaventa proclaims the possibility of living in freedom from this distorted quest for identity because of God's liberating triumph through Jesus Christ. "Galatians emerges as a powerful voice articulating God's new creation, a creation that liberates both women and men from their worlds of achievement and identity" (Gaventa 2000, 278).

Live out the reality that in Christ there is neither Jew nor Gentile, neither slave nor free, nor is there male and female. Let us live out the freedom Gaventa has just articulated. The implications of this section are clear yet challenging. I will make two brief observations. First, we must not limit ourselves to just this list of three couplets. What might Paul include in the list if he was writing to your church today? We will reflect further on that in the response section. Second, living this out is not a matter of human effort and willpower. It is good to ask, "How can I do better at treating with more dignity those in my church family that society has pushed me to look down upon?" But for many of us, it is important to first ask, "How can I more deeply experience the reality of my identity in Christ and thus be freer of societal definitions of identity?" The more secure we are in our identity as loved children of God, the freer we will be to welcome all others to the family table.

Do not deny differences. As Beverly Gaventa and John Barclay stated, union with Christ does not produce boring sameness. Paul still identifies as Jew and he writes to Gentiles. He is not advocating for a superficial colorblindness or genderlessness that papers over differences and does not necessarily heal the wounds of stratification and discrimination. As Connie Nicholson observes,

> If someone tells me that they're going to treat me as a man and ignore my femininity, is that supposed to be a compliment? How much more powerful (and empowering) is it to say, "I see your femininity, I don't want you to act like a man. I see your race, your social status, I see you." The power of being 'in-Christ' is not that our differences disappear, but that our identity and value is not in these AND that since our identity does not rest on these traits, we do not use our distinction as a means to oppress or belittle others. A Christ-centric community has the commonality of Jesus—He is the common denomin-

ator. It is a powerful statement when polar opposites hang out together because they are a testament to their shared Christ-denominator which launches them into relating to one another "in-Christ" as a family instead of through our lenses of distinction (Nicholson 2021).

Not fuzzy. Some might read Galatians 3:28 as an affirmation of universal inclusion and a fuzzy approach. It is more accurate to say Paul describes radical inclusion—radical in the sense that it is open to all regardless of their ethnicity, gender, or economic or social status. It is radical inclusion because there are not boundary line requirements one must meet. It is not, however, universal inclusion that says "It does not matter what you believe, what God or gods you are committed to, all are included, no distinctions are made." The words before, "you who were baptized into Christ have clothed yourselves with Christ" and the words at the end of the verse, "all are one *in Christ Jesus*," undermine any attempt to claim Paul as affirming a fuzzy church in this verse. The radical inclusivity Paul proclaims cannot be separated from Jesus Christ. There is a center and one's orientation to that center matters. Many today reject bounded group religiosity, but simply erase the lines and live as a fuzzy group. Let us be just as explicit and strong in challenging the bounded paradigm as Paul, and like Paul let us replace it with a centered paradigm—centered on Christ.

Personal Response

- Imagine you are explaining baptism to a new Christian or a seeker. What are ways you could explain it so the person would understand it in a centered way rather than a bounded way?

- What kind of people are unlikely to sit together at the same table in your church? Based on that re-write a version of Galatians 3:28 that Paul might write to your church today.

- Thinking more broadly than just your church, what are common ways in your context that people divide and distinguish themselves from others? What groups of people are commonly seen as inferior? Make a list of pairings as Paul does in Galatians 3:28?

- What steps might you take individually and as a church to root more deeply in your identity in Jesus Christ? Then, what steps might you take individually and as a church to give more dignity to those in your church who feel on the inferior side of a pairing you listed above?

CHAPTER NINE

Religion Enslaves, God Redeems

The Text: Galatians 4:1-5:1

⁴¹ What I am saying is that as long as an heir is underage, he is no different from a slave, although he owns the whole estate. ² The heir is subject to guardians and trustees until the time set by his father. ³ So also, when we were underage, we were in slavery under the elemental spiritual forces of the world. ⁴ But when the set time had fully come, God sent his Son, born of a woman, born under the law, ⁵ to redeem those under the law, that we might receive adoption to sonship. ⁶ Because you are his sons, God sent the Spirit of his Son into our hearts, the Spirit who calls out, "Abba, Father." ⁷ So you are no longer a slave, but God's child; and since you are his child, God has made you also an heir.

⁸ Formerly, when you did not know God, you were slaves to those who by nature are not gods. ⁹ But now that you know God—or rather are known by God—how is it that you are turning back to those weak and miserable forces? Do you wish to be enslaved by them all over again? ¹⁰ You are observing special days and months and seasons and years! ¹¹ I fear for you, that somehow I have wasted my efforts on you.

[12] I plead with you, brothers and sisters, become like me, for I became like you. You did me no wrong. [13] As you know, it was because of an illness that I first preached the gospel to you, [14] and even though my illness was a trial to you, you did not treat me with contempt or scorn. Instead, you welcomed me as if I were an angel of God, as if I were Christ Jesus himself. [15] Where, then, is your blessing of me now? I can testify that, if you could have done so, you would have torn out your eyes and given them to me. [16] Have I now become your enemy by telling you the truth?

[17] Those people are zealous to win you over, but for no good. What they want is to alienate you from us, so that you may have zeal for them. [18] It is fine to be zealous, provided the purpose is good, and to be so always, not just when I am with you. [19] My dear children, for whom I am again in the pains of childbirth until Christ is formed in you, [20] how I wish I could be with you now and change my tone, because I am perplexed about you!

[21] Tell me, you who want to be under the law, are you not aware of what the law says? [22] For it is written that Abraham had two sons, one by the slave woman and the other by the free woman. [23] His son by the slave woman was born according to the flesh, but his son by the free woman was born as the result of a divine promise.

[24] These things are being taken figuratively: The women represent two covenants. One covenant is from Mount Sinai and bears children who are to be slaves: This is Hagar. [25] Now Hagar stands for Mount Sinai in Arabia and corresponds to the present city of Jerusalem, because she is in slavery with her children. [26] But the Jerusalem that is above is free, and she is our mother. [27] For it is written:

"Be glad, barren woman,
you who never bore a child;
shout for joy and cry aloud,
you who were never in labor;
because more are the children of the desolate woman
than of her who has a husband."

[28]Now you, brothers and sisters, like Isaac, are children of promise. [29]At that time the son born according to the flesh persecuted the son born by the power of the Spirit. It is the same now. [30]But what does Scripture say? "Get rid of the slave woman and her son, for the slave woman's son will never share in the inheritance with the free woman's son." [31]Therefore, brothers and sisters, we are not children of the slave woman, but of the free woman.

[5:1]It is for freedom that Christ has set us free. Stand firm, then, and do not let yourselves be burdened again by a yoke of slavery.

The Flow and Form of the Text

This first part of this section (4:1-7) continues with themes from the previous chapter. Paul then shifts to a focus on the Galatians' past religious experience followed by deeply personal words of his relationship with them. Paul then returns to the story of Abraham but this time using it as an allegory. He ends with a clear and passionate declaration of freedom in Christ and an exhortation to stand firm and not submit again to the slavery of religion (5:1). These final lines flow from what has come before in the letter, specifically as the culmination of the portion starting in 3:1.

The Text Explained

In chapter two of this book, in the section "Religion in Galatians," we already explored some of the verses in the first part of this chapter—specifically the meaning of the word *stoicheia* (4:3, 9). I encourage you to review that section as part of your study of this chapter.

Redeemed and adopted through Christ (4:1-7). Paul continues to use the metaphors heir and guardian as he did at the end of chapter 3. He compares the time period of a son being under the control of the guardian to humans being enslaved by the spiritual power religion (*stoicheia*). As we observed (3:10-12) the law given by God was not enslaving, but taken up and used by the *stoicheia* it became enslaving bounded religiosity. In two compact verses Paul proclaims the liberative work of Christ through shorthand phrases that invite listeners into the full narrative of Jesus Christ (4:4-5). The first two phrases, "But when the set time had fully come, God sent his Son," communicate that it was a work of God, at God's initiative, at the time selected by God. They underscore a central theme of the letter: God's action contrasted with human action (1;1, 4, 11-12, 15-17; 2:16; 3:2-4). Divine action, yes, but the third phrase reminds the Galatians of the humanity of Jesus, "born of a woman." Paul signals that the life of Jesus, not just the cross, had importance. In combination with the next phrase, "born under the law," Paul emphasizes that Jesus as a human dealt with religious realities and pressures too. But he was not just any human, any Jew; in the final phrases Paul communicates that Jesus was the son of God sent by God to "to redeem those under the law, that we might receive adoption to sonship."

Let us use these four shorthand phrases as a door and pass through it to reflect on the narrative of Jesus and the law ("born of a woman, born under the law, to redeem those under the law, that we might receive adoption to sonship"). Jesus, day in and day out, observed people suffering under the weight of bounded group religiosity and seeking to remain within the lines. He also saw people shamed and excluded—on the wrong side of lines drawn by religious leaders. Jesus had seen and experienced things similar to what occurred in Antioch (2:11-13) and was happening in

Galatia. Jesus repeatedly confronted those drawing religious lines of exclusion and expressed love and acceptance to those on the wrong side of religious lines. Practicing a centered approach, he went against the spirit of religion and invited both the excluded and the excluders to table fellowship (for example, Luke 15). For all this Jesus himself experienced rejection and hostility from those practicing bounded group religiosity. As Paul wrote in chapter 3, Jesus suffered the curse of religious law, in the ultimate sense on the cross (3:13).

In Colossians Paul also wrote of the elemental spiritual powers (*stoicheia*) that used religious regulations to enslave (Colossians 2:8-9, 16, 20-23), and in that letter as well he presented the cross as a moment of confrontation of these powers. Through the cross the religious powers that had joined with other powers to kill Jesus were exposed and disarmed (Colossians 2:15). The power religion can put on garments, like the law, that give it the appearance of being of God, but through the cross and resurrection the outer garments were pulled off and the true character of this spiritual force was exposed.

In the shorthand phrases, Paul uses the terms "redeem" and "adoption" to describe the liberating work of the cross and resurrection. Paul's use of "redeem" may confuse some because it is not a word used commonly in day-to-day speech—at least not in the way Paul is using it. You may stop, stare, scratch your head, and wonder what he means. For others the problem is the opposite, it is such a common word in Christian discourse that you may not slow down at all to wonder what Paul communicates by this word. For many the word has become a synonym for "save"—which is not incorrect, but only scratches the surface. To include in the meaning of "redeem" a sense of buying is a helpful step, but without further explanation it may confuse more than clarify.

What might Paul have had in mind when he dictated that word? In the first-century world of Paul and the Galatians, and in the Old Testament, the word was commonly used in relation to freeing a slave. Often it included paying the slave's owner to release the slave, but not always. For instance in Exodus 6:6 God promises to redeem Israel from slavery in Egypt. There is no mention of payment at that time or later in the story. The word, however, was not limited just to liberating slaves. Boaz redeemed Ruth. Old Testament scholar Sandra Richter states,

> In Israel's tribal society redemption was the act of a patriarch who put his own resources on the line to ransom a family member who had been driven to the margins of society by poverty, who had been seized by an enemy against who he had no defense, who found themselves enslaved by the consequences of a faithless life. Redemption was the means by which a lost family member was restored to a place of security within the kinship circle (Richter 2008, 43).

When we looked at the word "justified" through an Old Testament lens (in chapter five), we saw it had a sense of inclusion in God's covenant community. So too here, we see that "redeem" is not just about an individual's status with God. For Paul the word likely included a sense of liberation from slavery to the religious expression of the law and also a sense of inclusion in the family of God—two central themes in his letter: freedom and inclusion. In terms of this commentary, we could say that Paul uses the word "redeem" to refer to Christ suffering the ultimate cost, the curse of religion (3:13), in our place. His redeeming act liberates us *from* bounded group religiosity and liberates us *for* kinship in God's family as expressed in a centered-church community.

Through this more in-depth understanding of "redeem" we see how closely it relates to the next phrase about adoption. Through Paul's use of "we" in verses 3 and 5 he includes himself, a Jew, as one enslaved by religion (*stoicheia*) and in need of Christ's liberating action through the cross. Take a moment and ponder how all those listening—Gentile Christians and Jewish-Christian missionaries—might have responded to Paul's startling statement that included himself, a Jew, in the category of adopted children.

In verse 6 Paul again makes very clear that he is, in the present tense, including the Galatians in the category of adopted children. They do not have to comply with certain Jewish practices in order to gain a seat at the family table, they *already* are part of the family (see also: 2:16; 3:2-3, 9, 22, 26, 29). Through the Spirit of Jesus they are able to address God as father in the intimate way Jesus did, "*Abba*" (see also Romans 8:15-17). How do they know whether they belong to God's family? Paul's answer has a relational and centered character: you know you are part of the family because you cry out to God as *Abba*, father.

In using the metaphor of adoption, in addition to continuing with themes of family and inheritance, Paul also highlights again the importance of identity (see the commentary on 3:6-14 in chapter 7). When a child is adopted, many things change in their life: they have new parents, a new name, new siblings, new inheritance, and new ways of practicing family life. It is a radical change of identity. This new identity of adopted children of God comes through and is rooted in the cross; it does not come through nor is it rooted in works of the law or ethnicity—neither for Jewish Christians nor Gentile Christians.

Appeal to restore a ruptured relationship (4:8-20). Paul changes tone and theme. After the positive proclamation of the previous verses, he turns to the sad current reality of the Galatian churches. What he just proclaimed is true, but they are not living according to that truth. A similarity with the previous section is that Paul continues to write about the enslaving actions of the *stoicheia* (here translated as "forces" [4:9]). As we observed in chapter two of this book, in a startling way Paul equates Judaism, paganism, and the line-drawing version of Christianity of the agitators. Paul is not saying they are the same thing. Rather, he is saying that they can all be used by *stoicheia* as tools of enslavement.

In verse 10 Paul mentions their celebrating certain special days as evidence of their return to religious ways (probably sabbath, new-moon festivals, Day of Atonement, Passover, and other Jewish festivals). We must be careful to not turn Paul into making a bounded group statement—the special-days group vs. the no-days-are-special group. In other places he writes of the first day of the week as a special day (I Corinthians 16:2) and refers to Jewish feast days (I Corinthians 16:8). In Romans he writes that each person can decide if a day is special or not (Romans 14:5-6). The problem is not the days or the celebrations themselves, but participating in them in a religious way—seeing them as a way of earning something from God or solidifying status within a bounded religious group.

Paul is perplexed by and concerned about their turn to the way of the other missionaries, their turn back to the ways of bounded group religion (4:9, 11). Why the turn? We already observed in chapter seven that in their honor-shame society they likely felt shamed by their neighbors for not participating in traditional religious activities like others. Turning back was a shame-avoiding move. In addition to social pressure to return to religious ways, they were immersed in an environment saturated with religious conceptions of the gods. Greeks and Romans believed they were at the mercy of spirits, powers, and the gods. People had great respect for their gods and also lived in fear of them. Their religious practices gave them means to appease the gods to avoid punishment and ways to please the gods in order to receive help. Having lived with that mindset for years before turning to Jesus, it could be easy to slide back into viewing God in this distorted religious way. The way the other missionaries talked about God and Jewish practices could have contributed to a return to old views. It may have felt not only familiar but also attractive.

Paul then becomes even more personal, in tone and content, pleading with them, addressing them as brothers and sisters, recalling their time together (4:12-16). Although Paul has expressed strong frustration with them (1:6; 3:1), he has not rejected them. He expresses his brotherly concern for his siblings. In the letter Paul practices what he suggests (6:1). He confronts not to exclude them in a bounded way, but to restore them according to a centered approach.

Paul entered into their Gentile world and became like them (4:12, see also 1 Corinthians 9:21). We can assume he ate with them as he did with Gentile Christians in Antioch (2:11-13). When Paul writes "become like me," he is not encouraging them to live like a Jew. Rather he is encouraging them to live in freedom from bounded religiosity as he does, to live in centered ways as he does.

In this paragraph Paul reminds them of their mutual relationship and pleads with them to remember it as they evaluate whether to go the way of the agitators or not. Expressing his emotions may well have had strategic value in persuading the Galatians. Let us, however, not make Paul all "head" and strategy. He likely expressed the emotions in this paragraph and in verses 19-20 because he really felt them, he truly longed to be with them, he recalled with fond appreciation their time together. Relationship and emotion are as much part of Paul's role of apostle as logical argument or teaching of doctrine.

In relation to verses 13-15, there is much here that we do not know. Paul does not go into detail because those receiving the letter know the details. We know that Paul had been with them in the past and preached the gospel. He arrived sick, or perhaps recovering from wounds of persecution. (Literally, the Greek is "weakness of the flesh" [4:13], thus it could be illness or wounds.) We know that his physical condition caused difficulties for the Galatians, but they welcomed him warmly and treated him well. They were willing to sacrifice to help him. (Although he may have had problems with his eyes, we should not assume that. The phrase in verse 15 was a common saying equivalent to "You would have given your right arm for me.") After reminding them of this, he ends by asking what has happened to all that good will and solidarity (4:16). This question sets up the turn to focus on the agitators. Implicit in the question is the reality that some are critical of Paul. Certainly the agitators are, and perhaps some of the Galatian Christians as well.

Referring to the other missionaries, Paul states, "Those people are zealous to win you over, but for no good" (4:17a). The word "zealous" was commonly used to refer to religious fervor—as when Paul described his zealousness for Judaism (1:14). It also was applied in the context of courting someone romantically, or courting a person's favor, and had the sense of earnestly desiring. We appropriately weave both those meanings into our reading of this phrase. The verse ends with the same Greek word. This literal translation captures well the symmetry of the verse:

> They are zealously-seeking you— not commend-
> ably, but they want to shut you out [or exclude you]

in-order-that you might be zealously-seeking them
(Disciples Literal New Testament).

Many find the latter half of the verse puzzling. Some translations, like the NIV, add the phrase "from us" ("What they want is to alienate you from us" [4:17b]). The NIV translators attempt to clarify what they assume Paul is saying—that the agitators are trying to shut the Galatians off from Paul so they will desire to be with the other missionaries. There is logic to that, but the words "from us" are not in the Greek text. Many translations do not add that phrase, but leave Paul's sentence as he wrote it, such as:

> They eagerly seek you, not in a commendable way,
> but they want to shut you out so that you will seek
> them (NASB).

> They make much of you, but for no good purpose;
> they want to exclude you, so that you may make
> much of them (NRSV).

We do better to follow the translations that do not add the extra words, "from us." The NIV's effort to make the logic of the verse clear actually pulls us away from more profound meaning and implications. The logic, and deeper meaning, becomes evident if we look at the verse through the lens of bounded group religiosity and view the exclusion in verse 17 like the exclusion in Antioch (2:11-14). The Jewish Christians from Jerusalem excluded the Gentile Christians from table fellowship in order to pressure them to live like Jews. Put yourself in the literal seats of those Gentile Christians and imagine the desire you would feel to be at the table with the in-crowd. Richard Hays writes, "Paul looks at the Galatian situation with psychological realism and sees that the exclusivity of the Jewish-Christian Missionaries makes their religious 'club' seem highly desirable to those who are on the outside" (Hays 2000, 295). To draw a line of exclusion, however, does more than just make those outside feel inferior and stir up motivation to comply with the line. The line also gives those inside a feeling of superiority—they gain honor. Again, with psychological realism Paul states "so that you may make much of them." He recognizes what it does for the insiders in a bounded group when outsiders take the group's lines seriously and seek to become insiders. It reinforces the sense of importance and veracity of the lines of the bounded group. The more people that obey the lines, the more power the lines have, and the more status and honor those inside the lines have. Thus, Paul warns the Galatians that the agitators' zealous pursuit is not, ultimately, out of concern for the Galatians but driven by concern for the bounded group itself and those in the group.

This verse is sharply critical of the agitators. Rather, however, than take the obvious step of concluding they were very bad people, we do much better to ask: how did this happen? How did sincere followers of Jesus seeking to do good, end up being so strongly critiqued by Paul? We do well to keep in mind the *stoicheia* and recognize that there is a spiritual force working within the bounded approach that overwhelms and distorts the motivations and purposes of the participants.

Paul ends this section as he began it, repeating that he is perplexed and expressing intimacy; now rather than brothers and sisters he says "dear children" (4:19) and ends with a surprising metaphor comparing himself to a mother giving birth. This not only communicates the depth of feeling and pain Paul has about this situation, the birth image also represents change. He writes with the hope and expectation that something will happen. For him this is not just a debate over doctrinal points. He hopes to see concrete changes in the churches and individuals. He hopes to see evidence of the reality of the new creation of Jesus Christ instead of evidence that shows they are living according to the present evil age enslaved by the *stoicheia* (1:4; 4:1-11; 6:15).

Allegory of Hagar and Sarah (4:21-5:1). The first verse in the section underscores the importance of humility and caution whenever we say, "this is what Paul means by 'the law.'" He uses the word in two different ways in the same verse. He applies "under the law" to those in Galatia who are taking up the Jewish practices the other missionaries are pressing upon them, but when he writes "what the law says" he is referring to Scripture, in this case specifically Genesis—which does not include the laws and commands given by God to Israel. For clarity in this sentence, "Scripture" would seem to be the better word. Perhaps he uses "law" because he knows the agitators are referring to the law a great deal—both in the sense of laws given to Israel and referring to Scripture as "the law." Paul wants to argue from the same basis. That helps us understand why he works so hard to use a story the other missionaries also probably relied on.

If we read this section as a historical narrative, we could spend a lot of time trying to get it to fit with the biblical account, and still not succeed. (Where, for instance, do we find the connection Paul states between Hagar and Mt. Sinai or Jerusalem?) Paul does not pretend to be making an argument from history. He states he is using historical figures in an allegorical way (4:24). An allegory uses one thing to represent another. Allegorical interpretation was common in Paul's time.

There are a number of details we could speculate about. When Paul places the present Jerusalem in the slavery category represented by Hagar and Ishmael, for instance, is he referring to

Judaism or to the bounded group Jewish Christians in Jerusalem? Instead we will focus on how Paul lines up the different characters and entities through this chart and then the points he makes in conclusion.

SLAVE	FREE
Hagar	Sarah
Ishmael	Isaac
Human decision/Flesh	Divine promise/Spirit
Covenant of Mt Sinai/Jerusalem	Covenant Heavenly Jerusalem
Other missionaries	Galatian Gentile Christians

Paul forcefully makes two points. First, he clearly includes the Galatian Christians as children of the Free, heirs of the promise. In relation to our chart, Paul is communicating, "You are already in the right column!" Second, he links the allegory to the rest of the letter, stating: "It is for freedom that Christ has set us free" (5:1). These words culminate not just the theological argument from 3:1, but all of the letter to this point. Paul sandwiches these indicative statements of the reality of their freedom in Christ between two similar imperatives. Paul uses Sarah's words to Abraham, "Get rid of the slave woman and her son" (4:30; Genesis 21:10) as an implicit command to get rid of the agitators, or at least to get rid of their enslaving system. Paul repeats that command in the other half of the sandwich. On the basis of their freedom in Christ he commands them, "Stand firm, then, and do not let yourselves be burdened again by a yoke of slavery."

These final words combined with the allegorical command to get rid of the slave woman appear to tell the Galatians to disassociate from the agitators. Does Paul actually mean to break fellowship and exclude them? Perhaps he is not thinking of people, but the bounded paradigm, "get rid of it!" Yet purging the Galatian churches of bounded group religiosity may have to include separating from some individuals if they are unwilling to leave their line-drawing ways. Some readers may wonder, "does not Paul then become bounded himself?" To answer that question let us step away from Paul and Galatia for a moment and deepen our understanding of bounded and centered through an analogy with soccer.

A league soccer team is a bounded group. There are tryouts. Ability matters. A team also has other requirements, such as having a uniform, attending practices, paying dues to the league, and so on. Coaches draw a clear line to determine which players have the ability and meet the requirements to be on the team. Others are turned away; they are not on the team. It is analogous to the bounded religious group in Antioch that communicated, "you cannot eat with us unless you meet the requirements—live like a Jew." In relation to soccer, a centered approach would be when a group invites anyone who wants to play soccer to gather at a local park on Saturday afternoon at three o'clock. All who show up are included. In terms of the centered group diagram (chapter one), their showing up displays they are interested in soccer. Their arrows are heading toward the center, soccer. Those who do not show up to play are represented by the people whose arrows are turned away from the center. Some of those who show up may not be very good, but their lack of ability will not exclude them. If too many people show up, the organizers will start another game. As in a centered church, if they have turned toward the center they are included.

Now, let's imagine that the centered-approach soccer players have gathered and are playing. What will happen if one person picks up the ball and runs with it? The others will say, "You can't do that. This is not rugby." If the person continues to grab the ball, the others will say that this person cannot participate until they are willing to play by the rules of soccer. If they set the rules aside they would no longer be playing soccer. They would not be centered on soccer. In terms of the diagram the player who refuses to stop using her hands has turned her arrow away from soccer, the center.*

As we turn back to Paul and Galatians, it is important to note that the person who keeps picking up the ball ruins the game for everyone. They tell this person to play by the rules or leave for the good of all. To tell the player to leave does not stop the group from being centered; it is, in fact, part of their being a centered group. For similar reasons Paul tells the Galatians to separate from the agitators, not just because these other missionaries are off track, but because their turn from the gospel, the center, is hurting others. It is important to note in both Paul's case and the centered soccer analogy, the first move is not separation but correction. Paul confronted Peter in Antioch. He sought to reorient him; Paul did not tell him to leave the church. Of course, in a centered approach even if it comes to the point of needing separation, the goal is restoration; a reoriented person will be welcomed back. In the commentary on Galatians 6:1 we will reflect more on how centered confrontation differs from bounded.

---

* This analogy is taken from, and is further developed in my book, *Centered-Set Church*, 21, 24, 47-48.

We will end by returning to the meat of the sandwich, "For freedom Christ has set us free" (5:1). What makes Paul, and a centered church, centered is not first and foremost avoiding line-drawing to define who belongs; rather, it is the focus on and proclamation of God's work through Jesus Christ. It is through God's action that the Galatians have a place at the table of God's family and are free of the elemental spiritual forces such as bounded group religiosity.

Implications of the Text for Today

Principalities and powers. These words from Ephesians 6:12 capture well a clear implication of this section of Paul's letter: "For our struggle is not against flesh and blood, but against the rulers, against the authorities, against the powers of this dark world and against the spiritual forces of evil in the heavenly realms." We must recognize that as helpful as diagrams and explanations of bounded, fuzzy, and centered might be, they are not enough. True liberation from the enslaving *stoicheia* comes through Jesus Christ, and we must rely on the Holy Spirit in an ongoing way as we seek to resist the power of bounded group religiosity.

Not just a few bad agitators. It could be easy to view a few especially bounded people as the problem. If we do so we tend to put ourselves in the category of good centered Christians and not be self-critical. An important implication that flows from the previous one is recognizing that the fundamental problem is enslaving spiritual forces and we all must be vigilant against ways we can get sucked into their divisive religious ways. Rather than assume we are fine, better to assume we are like the Galatians and look for ways we might be "turning back" as well.

Active resistance. To say it is not just a few bad agitators, does not mean there are not people who are especially problematic and actively suck others into religious ways. Throughout the letter, and in this section particularly, Paul takes an active stance. He confronts the religiosity of others, he warns of the power religion, warns against problematic religious agitators, and encourages strong decisive action be taken against the enslaving power and its human agents. Let us follow Paul's example.

Alternative security. Although bounded religiosity sows division, hinders authenticity, spreads shame, and weighs people down with demands, it does provide status, a sense of belonging, and security. I speculated that shame avoidance and a desire for security and status is part of what may have pulled the Galatian Christians to turn back to religious ways. As we take an active stance and seek to dismantle bounded group religiosity, we must be sensitive to the reality that people will lose this form of security and status in the process. If we do not replace it, people will easily be pulled back into religion. The security and status provided by a centered church, however, are radically different. Although superficially the security that comes through a centered relationship may not be as comfortable or feel as secure as what religion provides, it is a deep security. It is healthy and it provides status, or perhaps better to say dignity, which does not depend on putting others down. Note how Paul intentionally acts to restore and buttress the Galatian Christians' sense of security and dignity in Christ, saying things like: "You are children of God," "You are heirs," "You are children of the promise." Let us also look for ways to do the same.

Personal Response

- Are there ways you will think differently now when you encounter the word "redeem" in the Bible? Take a few moments to reflect on the present significance for you of being redeemed by Jesus Christ?

- What are ways the *stoicheia* may be seeking to take up your beliefs and practices and use them as tools of religiosity?

- Does observing Paul's expression of emotions, and his focus on relationship and longing to be with the Galatians, change the way you think about him? Does it change the way you think about the role of a mentor, pastor, discipler?

- Have you been involved in, or observed, confrontation of a church leader for being too bounded, too religious? Do you think that type of confrontation is done as much as Paul would in your context? Reflect on some instances when you think it was/is needed and how it might be addressed in a centered way?

- Reflect on what the Holy Spirit might be saying to you through this statement and exhortation by Paul: "It is for freedom that Christ has set us free. Stand firm, then, and do not let yourselves be burdened again by a yoke of slavery" (5:1).

CHAPTER TEN

Freedom to Love

The Text: Galatians 5:2-26

² *Mark my words! I, Paul, tell you that if you let yourselves be circumcised, Christ will be of no value to you at all.* ³ *Again I declare to every man who lets himself be circumcised that he is obligated to obey the whole law.* ⁴ *You who are trying to be justified by the law have been alienated from Christ; you have fallen away from grace.* ⁵ *For through the Spirit we eagerly await by faith the righteousness for which we hope.* ⁶ *For in Christ Jesus neither circumcision nor uncircumcision has any value. The only thing that counts is faith expressing itself through love.*

⁷ *You were running a good race. Who cut in on you to keep you from obeying the truth?* ⁸ *That kind of persuasion does not come from the one who calls you.* ⁹ *"A little yeast works through the whole batch of dough."* ¹⁰ *I am confident in the Lord that you will take no other view. The one who is throwing you into confusion, whoever that may be, will have to pay the penalty.* ¹¹ *Brothers and sisters, if I am still preaching circumcision, why am I still being persecuted? In that case the offense of the cross has been abolished.* ¹² *As for those agitators, I wish they would go the whole way and emasculate themselves!*

13 You, my brothers and sisters, were called to be free. But do not use your freedom to indulge the flesh [a]; rather, serve one another humbly in love. 14 For the entire law is fulfilled in keeping this one command: "Love your neighbor as yourself." [b] 15 If you bite and devour each other, watch out or you will be destroyed by each other.

16 So I say, walk by the Spirit, and you will not gratify the desires of the flesh. 17 For the flesh desires what is contrary to the Spirit, and the Spirit what is contrary to the flesh. They are in conflict with each other, so that you are not to do whatever [c] you want. 18 But if you are led by the Spirit, you are not under the law.

19 The acts of the flesh are obvious: sexual immorality, impurity and debauchery; 20 idolatry and witchcraft; hatred, discord, jealousy, fits of rage, selfish ambition, dissensions, factions 21 and envy; drunkenness, orgies, and the like. I warn you, as I did before, that those who live like this will not inherit the kingdom of God.

22 But the fruit of the Spirit is love, joy, peace, forbearance, kindness, goodness, faithfulness, 23 gentleness and self-control. Against such things there is no law. 24 Those who belong to Christ Jesus have crucified the flesh with its passions and desires. 25 Since we live by the Spirit, let us keep in step with the Spirit. 26 Let us not become conceited, provoking and envying each other.

---

a. Galatians 5:13 In contexts like this, the Greek word for flesh (sarx) refers to the sinful state of human beings, often presented as a power in opposition to the Spirit; also in verses 16, 17, 19 and 24; and in 6:8.

b. Galatians 5:14 Lev. 19:18

c. Galatians 5:17 Or you do not do what

The Flow and Form of the Text

This section marks a significant change in the letter, a shift from a theological argument about who belongs in the Christian community and why, to a focus on actions of those in the community. The first verses focus on an action, circumcision, at the heart of the discussion of identity and community membership in the previous chapters. In verse 13 Paul widens the discussion from one specific action to a broader discussion of Christian ethics. It continues through the section explored in the next chapter of this book. Some see this part of the letter (5:13-6:10) as so distinct from the rest of Galatians that they conclude Paul must have been addressing two separate problems—first, individuals with a poor understanding of grace and an overemphasis on works, and second, loose-living individuals with little to no emphasis on Christian ethics. Others find the two parts of the letter so incongruent that they speculate that this is a piece of another letter inserted later by an editor. If we imagine that Paul wrote the letter to correct a mistaken teaching of salvation by works, then yes, it does seem strange that he would spend more than a chapter writing about the importance of Christian ethical actions. What happens, however, when we look at the ethical emphasis in chapters 5 and 6 through the lens of what this commentary has argued motivated Paul to write the letter—a concern for the unity and health of the Christian community? Through that lens we see this material is closely related to the rest of the letter.

Just as Paul did not write the previous chapters thinking primarily of individuals, he does not, first and foremost have individuals in mind here. He did not write these verses to give a list of do's and don'ts for individual Christians. This a communal ethic. This section (5:2-6:10) has a communal focus in two ways. First, many of the imperatives are directed to the church community; the "you" in the commands is plural. Second, even when he does write about individual actions, they are actions that impact others in the church. In the first four chapters of the letter we observe Paul working to prevent division of the church community. These two chapters continue that theme and add to it material on living in harmony together.

Another way these two chapters are related to the rest of the letter is through offering a contrast to what Paul has critiqued. He critiqued the way the agitators talked about Christian behavior in a bounded way; now he models talking about it in a centered way.

Again, picturing the letter to the Galatians as tethered to the two poles, 1:4 and 6:15, we can say Paul not only proclaims freedom *from* the enslaving power of bounded group religiosity, he also proclaims freedom *for* new creation living. These chapters provide guidance in living out that freedom.

The Text Explained

A call to reject circumcision (5:2-6). Paul again uses attention grabbing words: "If you let yourselves be circumcised, Christ will be of no value to you at all" (5:2). The content is shocking and sobering enough, but Paul heightens the impact of the words by vesting them with the authority of his name, and first saying "Listen!" or "Mark my words!" He wants to make sure the Galatians know he means them. We can imagine some of the listeners thinking, "Wait a minute Paul, maybe we have put too much emphasis on Jewish traditions, but we still have faith in Christ. Aren't you overreacting?" As Paul will soon make clear (5:6; 6:15), it is not circumcision itself that makes Christ of no value, it is the bounded group context in which they would practice circumcision. If they accept circumcision as a religious dividing line the Galatians would return to the "present evil age" (1:4; 4:8-9). Rather than living in the freedom they have through Jesus Christ (5:1) they would be reconstructing the walls he had torn down (3:28).

In verse 3 he makes clear if they go the way of the other missionaries they will have to accept and practice not just circumcision but the whole system. As I explained in more detail in relation to 3:10-14, Paul is not saying one would have to obey all the laws without fail in order to be saved. Neither the other missionaries nor the Old Testament said that. Paul communicates that if they get circumcised, their identity will rest in works of the law, which differentiated Jews from Gentiles, rather than in the faithfulness of Jesus. Or, in terms of this commentary, it is a contrast between a bounded group that builds its identity on a line that distinguishes them from others and a centered group that builds its identity on their relationship with the center—Jesus. If the Galatian Christians accept the bounded group's line as the basis of their identity they will have to comply with all that is in that line—everything the group uses to distinguish itself as separate and superior. If they comply with some aspects and not others they will remain excluded outsiders. (For more on identity and works of the law, see chapter 5, "works of the law" and chapter 7, commentary on 3:6-12.)

It is not, however, just about having to comply with the practices emphasized by the other missionaries. A bounded church has a different character out of sync with Jesus. We feel this in verse 4. If they get circumcised and seek justification through the bounded group way of the agitators, they will leave the environment of grace and live in the environment of religion. In verse 5 Paul presents the contrasting option—through faith we have security and hope in God. Paul's emphasis on God's action is so strong that he even roots human faith as "through the Spirit" (5:4). Through the work of God, rather than works of the law, it is possible to follow another way. Note the already-but-not-yet character of this verse, present in other Pauline letters (Romans 8:18-26; I Corinthians 1:7; Philippians 3:20).

Imagine the listeners' surprise after hearing his strong words against circumcision when he now states "neither circumcision nor uncircumcision has any value" (5:6). Is he contradicting himself?

No. Paul is aware of the human propensity to use religious line drawing as a means to grasp for status superiority. He wants to make very clear he is not setting up a new anti-circumcision bounded group to counter the agitators' circumcision bounded group. The problem is not circumcision, it is bounded group religiosity. Paul's concern is a church putting their identity in something other than Jesus Christ. In that sense those of the un-circumcision group would be as off track as those of the circumcision group. For those in Christ neither circumcision nor uncircumcision have value as identity markers—they are not needed. (I suggest reviewing the section on "in Christ" in chapter six and thinking about how it relates to Paul's statement here.) Note the parallelism with Galatians 3:28; just as there, Paul is not denying the reality that there are circumcised and uncircumcised, slaves and free, men and women, but a centered church will not exclude one group or the other nor make one superior to the other.

The second part of the verse (5:6) relates to the discussion in "The Flow and Form of the Text" section. If one thinks that the main reason Paul wrote the letter was to emphasize grace and faith over against works then this verse, where he blends them together is confusing. That is not the case. He stands against works used as part of a bounded church's line of distinction but affirms loving actions flowing from a relationship of trust in Jesus Christ. The incident in Antioch gives concrete examples of these two types of works (2:11-14). Paul critiques the use of "works of the law" to exclude, shame, and cause division. He affirms the loving action of taking a seat at the table with the excluded. Paul's previous use of the word "love" in the letter points to the ultimate example of faith expressing itself through love, the faithful loving action of Jesus giving himself for us (2:20). Richard Hays states, "The church is called to embody this faith working through love in a way that corresponds to the story of the cross. The demand for circumcision is completely irrelevant to this calling" (Hays 2000, 314).

The agitators and the offense of the cross (5:7-12). Paul uses a sports analogy to communicate that they were doing well. What happened? He puts the blame, not on them, but on the runner who cut in on them (5:7). The question of who threw them off their pace is rhetorical. All those listening know he is referring to the other missionaries and their new teaching. Note that here, as in Galatians 2:5 and 2:14, truth for Paul is not just a proposition to affirm, it is something to live out. As at Antioch (2:11-14), previously the Galatian Christians had been living out new creation realities in Christ that were expressed in unity and love for others (6:15, 5:6). But that loving unity has been disrupted by the yeast of the bounded approach introduced by the agitators (5:9). One bump from another runner can ruin a race, a bit of yeast spreads through all of the dough.

These verses are quite condensed, but Paul's use of the same yeast metaphor in I Corinthians 5:6-7, where he states explicitly to get rid of problematic yeast, can help us read between the lines. Richard Hays offers this expanded paraphrase of Galatians 5:7-10, with the added explanation in italics:

> You were running well. Who cut in on you *and knocked you off balance,* to keep you from obeying the truth? Their elaborate rhetoric does not come from God who calls you; *if you listen to them they will lead you astray. Therefore, you must drive them out of your community,* because a little leaven leavens the whole lump of dough. *If you let them stay in your midst, they will corrupt the entire church.* I am confident in the

Lord that you will not think otherwise, *and that you will do as I say. Even if this sounds harsh, it is a matter of God's judgement.* Anyone who tries to confuse you will bear the judgement, whoever he may be (Hays 2000, 315).

Continuing his focus on the other missionaries, and continuing to require us to fill in details, in verse 11 Paul appears to respond to an ironic accusation that he himself advocated for circumcision. Perhaps the agitators were twisting things he had done or said elsewhere to imply he now also would preach the same thing as the agitators. Paul thinks this is ridiculous and as evidence he points to his ongoing persecution and the scandal of the cross. Jesus Christ was crucified in part because he offended the religious leaders by tearing down religious walls of separation. Jesus confronted their bounded ways of seeking status and honor, and they reacted with the act of extreme shaming—crucifixion. To preach circumcision as a badge of honor required to fully belong to the people of God goes the way of the crucifiers rather than the way of Jesus Christ the crucified. Paul's preaching and the cross continue to offend (I Corinthians 1:18-2:5), therefore, his point is that this accusation of theirs is obviously false.

It appears that this ridiculous false accusation and the thought of their corrupting yeast has again stirred Paul's passion (cf. 1:6-9; 3:1). In a sarcastic way he refers to circumcision but now as a curse against the agitators.

Free to serve with love (5:13-15). Those entrenched in a bounded approach often resist a centered approach because they mistake it for fuzzy approach. They think that without clearly drawn boundary lines people will do whatever they want. It is likely that the other missionaries felt something similar. Concerned that the Galatians would stray into all kinds of sin, the missionaries warned them about Paul's gospel of freedom. In these verses, and continuing through 6:10, Paul makes clear that he is not fuzzy. A centered approach includes clear statements of appropriate and inappropriate behavior. Yet as Paul also makes clear in these verses and those that follow, rather than trusting in drawn lines to control behavior Paul trusts in the Spirit; rather than commands rooted in a line of distinction that devolve into status competition, Paul roots commands in love.

Freedom is a central theme in the letter, but it is freedom from the powers of the present evil age (1:4). It is not an independence to do whatever you want. In individualistic societies people often interpret freedom as independence. Looking back on my life I can see actions I characterized as steps of freedom, but they were not what Paul had in mind when he used the word freedom. For instance, for a time I was an independent missionary. I framed it positively as freedom, but actually I wanted to avoid limitations being placed on my independence to act as I wanted. True, there were limitations to my independence when I joined a mission team, but I gained so much that I had been missing. I gave up independence, I did not, however, lose the sort of freedom Paul writes about. For him, freedom does not lessen our commitment and responsibility to others, nor to the law, rather it increases our ability to serve others in love and more thoroughly fulfill the law.

Paul, however, is about much more than just defending what I have called a centered approach and stating, "We take ethics seriously too." Rather, continuing with his impassioned concern for the health of the community—and the individuals in the church community—in verse 15 he exposes an ethical shortcoming of the way of the agitators. The combination of the agitators bounded religiosity and the competitive honor system of the day leads to people being shamed. To rise up they put others down. Even those on the inside of the lines live under the threat of losing their status. The way of the Spirit, the way of love, is superior.

Works of the flesh and fruit of the Spirit (5:16-26). Many of us, shaped by individualistic societies, most naturally read these verses as a list of dos and don'ts for individual Christians. Instead, let us imagine that Paul writes these verses with the same passionate concern for the church community as the rest of the letter. To read the verses through a community lens rather than an individual lens brings two significant changes. First, we will think not just of individuals being kind or of avoiding discord, but of the group as a whole doing so. Second, we will recognize the impact, positive or negative, on the community, of all the things listed. Meaning that through a community lens, even with the more individual actions like envy or fits of rage, we will think about their wider impact. Reading with a community emphasis does not rule out implications for individual behavior, but leads us to see more than that. Before you continue I encourage you to read these verses (5:16-26) twice, first with an individualistic lens and then with a community lens. How does it change how you see and interpret the same words?

Too often the Greek word in these verses literally translated as "flesh" is interpreted, or even translated, as referring to individual desires or a sinful part of individual humans. We do well to let the letter as a whole guide our interpretation of Paul's use of "flesh" in this section. The contrast between flesh and Spirit is parallel to the contrast between present evil age and new creation; between human action and the divine action; and between enslaving religiosity (*stoichea*) and freedom/truth of the gospel. As Eduardo Arens observes, "Spirit and flesh are not components of human nature, rather they are 'forces' humans base their lives on. They orient their lives 'according to the flesh' or 'according to the Spirit'" (Arens 2009, 206).* Similarly John Barclay writes that "Paul is not concerned here with a 'fleshy' part of each individual, but with the influence of an 'era' and its human traditions and assumptions.... The Spirit is... the divine power unleashed in the dawning of the new age, the source of new life" (Barclay 1988, 213). Building on the interpretations of these scholars, we can say that in terms of this commentary the flesh includes bounded group religiosity, distorted concepts of honor, and ethnic imperialism, but as their broad definitions imply the flesh is not limited to those things.

Paul states clearly that the flesh and the Spirit "are in conflict with each other" (5:17). The opposition is mutual. The flesh hinders the expression of the fruit of the Spirit, and the Spirit actively blocks or undermines the works of the flesh. Thinking in concrete examples from the letter, if the church walks by the Spirit there is no place for status games or discrimination between the rich and the poor or between ethnic groups (3:28). If the church lives by the Spirit of God, the fleshly power religion will not be able to draw lines of distinction that disrupt the harmony of united table fellowship (2:11-16).

The other missionaries have likely said that the Galatians need law for clarity in regard to Christian behavior, but Paul states the acts of the flesh are obvious (5:18-19). Paul then gives not a complete list, but some examples of things that are inappropriate or destructive behaviors (5:19-21). That is not to say it is a random list. Note that more than half the things mentioned would undermine the harmony and unity of the Christian community. He ends this

---

* My translation.

list with by repeating a warning he had said to them before, "those that live like this will not inherit the kingdom of God" (5:21). The word "inherit" gives an eschatological sense to the phrase and connects it to the theme of inheritance of chapters three and four. Richard Hays observes that the other missionaries "have taught that circumcision is necessary to inherit the kingdom. Paul, by contrast, indicates that one is excluded from the inheritance by these flesh-driven, community-splitting behaviors—precisely the outcomes produced, in his view, by the politics of the circumcision faction (2:11-14; 4:17; 5:15, 26; 6:13)" (Hays 2000, 327).

Paul's warning makes a clear connection between behavior and inheriting the kingdom of God (5:21). One might ask how the apostle of grace can talk about actions in that way. Or, perhaps, how is that not a bounded-church statement? First, note that Paul does not say, "if you do any of those things you are out." It is not that a single infraction puts you on the wrong side of the line. Rather he says, "who live like this." He is referring to continuing action over time. To ask the above questions about Paul has more to do with the questioner having a concept of grace with no sense of reciprocity than with any inconsistency in Paul. In chapter three of this book, in the section on grace, I explained that thinking of a true gift as having no expectation of something being given in return, is relatively recent; and even today is not universal in all cultures. The radicalness of Paul's understanding of God's grace was not the lack of expectation of response. Rather, in a context in which people constantly evaluated people's status and only gave gifts to those they deemed worthy, Paul proclaimed God gives regardless of someone's status or worth. To say that one had done nothing to merit receiving God's grace would not, at that time, rule out talking about actions expected in response to the gift. Obedience as reciprocity would not have conflicted with Paul's understanding of grace.

As we saw in the first verses of Galatians chapter three, they did not receive the Spirit because of works; that was grace. Here Paul communicates that those who have received the Spirit will be transformed. They will not practice the works of the flesh, but will produce the fruit of the Spirit. In a centered church one's behavior does not earn entrance into the community, but relationship with the center will change behavior. If someone in a centered church began living in ways listed in verses 19-21 it would reveal they had turned from the center and need reorientation—the sort of thing Paul will address in Galatians 6:1.

"The fruit of the Spirit is love, joy, peace, forbearance, kindness, goodness, faithfulness, gentleness and self-control" (5:22-23). When I read that list my natural inclination is to think of an individual displaying those characteristics. Once again, we must remember that Paul was not an individualistic North American and he is writing this letter out of concern for the harmony and unity of the community. That does not mean he would oppose applying this list to individuals, but it does mean he likely would oppose applying it *only* to individuals.

The list is communal in three ways. First, Paul invites us to think of a church as a group exhibiting gentleness or kindness or exuding peace or joy. Of course, for the church to manifest these qualities as a group, individuals will have to practice them at a personal level. Again, the point is neither an individual nor a communal reading, but both. Second, expression of these qualities will contribute to group harmony in contrast to the works of the flesh that disrupt and divide. Third, even if we focus on individuals displaying the fruit, most of them cannot be done alone. They are relational, expressed to others or with others in the community.

This communal character is true even in a fruit like self-control. My friend, and New Testament scholar, Ross Wagner helped me see this. First, he observed that "self" does not have to be in the translation of the Greek word. "Forbearance" is another possible translation. Ross also encouraged me to think about forbearance/self-control in relation the previous list (5:19-21)—especially the last two: drunkenness, carousing. Imagine a drunken party, or a group expressing hate-filled political outrage—in person or online. What is going on? It is not just lack of individual restraint. Group excess encourages individuals to overindulge. They feed off each other. More individual lack of restraint increases the level of group carousing which leads to greater individual lack of restraint. Since Paul mentioned these words on carousing just before, it is quite appropriate to think that when he wrote that self-control is a fruit of the Spirit he was thinking of it in both a group and individual way. Works of the flesh: drunkenness, revelry, group carousing stand in contrast to fruit of the Spirit: temperance, moderation—a very different image of a group activity.

As we have seen repeatedly in Galatians, here too God is the primary actor. The Spirit produces the fruit. That does not mean humans are passive. In this same letter Paul urges the Galatians to act, to work at these things (5:25; 6:4, 9-10). Perhaps thinking of an actual fruit tree is helpful. We cannot produce the fruit, but we can prune and put compost around the tree which will aid in the growth of these virtues in our lives and in our congregations.

Love is first in the list and has already been highlighted by Paul as fundamental (5:13-14). It will influence all else. The actions and attitudes of the agitators in Galatia will not create an environment of love. The Gentile believers in Antioch certainly did not feel loved by the Jerusalem visitors (2:11-14). The bounded approach did not foster peace. Paul opts for a centered approach. Rather than drawing a new line with a different set of rules and laws, he presents a list of virtues that are the result of centering on Jesus and walking with the Spirit.

In the rest of verse 23 and verse 24 Paul confronts the bounded group stance of the agitators in two ways. First, he pulls it out of the context of a law discussion by stating there is no law against these virtues. Second, whereas the agitators likely advocated for the need for laws to prevent moral chaos, Paul points to being united with Christ as bringing order.

After the two descriptive lists that we might describe as implicit commands, in verse 25 Paul turns to a direct imperative. It is rooted in an indicative statement of who they are, similar to other statements in the chapter linking an indicative with an imperative (5:1; 5:13) (indicative: "Since we live by the Spirit;" imperative: "Let us keep in step with the Spirit"). Note, the directional nature of the command. Rather than a line-drawing command, "let us demonstrate we are true people of the Spirit by complying with these requirements," Paul's command has a sense of journey, of progressing. It is both less threatening than a bounded approach, but at the same time more demanding. It is not, "do this and you are in." It is: keep walking; in an ongoing way continue to stay in step with the Spirit. One is about crossing a line; the other is about following a line toward the center.

Paul's second command, verse 26, is in line with the first. He makes the positive statement of what to do, walk with the Spirit in a centered way, then what to avoid—the status grabbing bounded approach. The first fosters harmony, the second competition and disharmony.

Implications of the Text for Today

Respond to human religious tendencies with intentionality.
Paul is aware of how easily we slide back into bounded approaches.
He knows that after his strong critique of circumcision many will
naturally draw a line using uncircumcision as a defining characteristic. He does not assume that because of all he has already
proclaimed in the letter they will not go the religious way. Rather
he makes the surprising, to religious ears, statement "that in Christ
Jesus neither circumcision nor uncircumcision has any value"
(5:6). Paul with intentionality undercuts the human tendency to
gain a sense of being "in" by defining others as "out," to gain status
by putting others down, and to gain a sense of worth before God
through "right" behavior. Let us be as intentional.

**Insufficiency of viewing the problem as incorrect teaching,
part 1.** As we get deeper into Paul's letter to the Galatians the
weaknesses of understanding the problem in Galatia as an incorrect
teaching on works becomes more apparent. Teaching salvation by
grace, not works, is correct, but it is not enough. Simply stating
correct information is not enough. It alone does not counter the
spiritual powers' (*stoichea*) enslaving actions that take advantage of
humans' natural tendency to grasp for status and security through
line-drawing religiosity. If we think the problem is incorrect doctrinal
information, we can live in the illusion that we are safe because
we have correct doctrine. Yet, as I recount in the first chapter of
my book, *Centered-Set Church*, for years I proclaimed salvation by
grace, but lived as if I was saved by works. I measured myself and
others according to lines I had drawn. It was not until I recognized
the depth of my enslavement to religion and received a stronger
dose of the liberating gospel of Jesus Christ that I truly lived out
the grace I had proclaimed.

It is appropriate to communicate to followers of Jesus expectations of changed behavior. The presence of this section of the letter, and the one to follow, display that Paul did not consider it problematic to have expectations of changed behavior. Nor did he consider it problematic to state examples of appropriate and inappropriate behavior and character traits. The problem was linking behavior and status by using behavior as a standard in a bounded-church way. A number of factors have contributed to a distortion of the place of works in the Christian life, including what is described in the section that follows.

Insufficiency of Viewing the problem as incorrect teaching, part 2. The misdiagnosis of the problem in Galatia and over-confidence in the efficacy of stating salvation is by grace, not works, often leads to a situation even more twisted and ironic than what is stated above in part 1. Thinking that stating salvation is not by works is the most important thing Paul does, combined with a modern Western understanding of grace as being a gift with no expectation of response, leads to a distorted understanding of works. It leaves people wary of talking about works at all. They do not want to teach or preach something that might even imply the necessity of human action. Thus, as described at the beginning of this chapter, some struggle to see how this section of Galatians is even part of the same letter. So at one level, as described above, the emphasis on stating salvation is by grace does not actually prevent living out works righteousness, at another level it hinders people from having a healthy understanding of the centrality of behavior in the life of a disciple of Jesus Christ. But, as described in chapter three of this book, this is based on a misunderstanding of grace. What happens if rather than seeing the radicalness of God's grace in its total lack of an expectation of reciprocal action, we see it in God's gift showered on people regardless of their worth? Then it is not just acceptable to talk about Christian actions as Paul does, it is actually an integral part of proclaiming God's grace. As John Barclay states, "[God's grace was] given in order to transform the recipients and to establish a permanent relationship; the receipt of this gift is necessarily expressed in gratitude, obedience, and transformed behavior" (Barclay 2020, 149). It does not contaminate or weaken the message of grace to speak of expected behavioral change if we think about grace the way Paul presents it.

In addition, to interpret justification only in terms of the individual's relationship with God can lead some to experience any talk of appropriate actions as bounded religion. In contrast, to have a broader definition of justification that also contains a sense of inclusion in the people of God contributes to a centered understanding. From this perspective, talk of works is not incompatible with justification through trusting in Jesus' saving work; rather, talk of works can have the sense of family expectations. In a healthy family, rather than a sense of getting in, or gaining status through behavior, there is a sense of: this is the way we live in this family we are part of.

Therefore, let us, like Paul, proclaim that by God's gracious initiative through Jesus we have worth, are included in God's family, and are freed from the necessity of using actions as a means of gaining status. This enables us to talk of living in line with the Spirit as an appropriate and expected response to the grace we have received. Grace understood in this way, far from prohibiting talk of the importance of avoiding certain actions (5:19-21) and of cultivating positive virtues (5:22-24) enables us to join Paul in strongly emphasizing them. The God of grace calls us to this response. It is an integral part of becoming more fully the loving new creation community freed from status accrual through the cross of Christ.

A call to individual and corporate cultivation of the fruit of the Spirit. Let us not only think individually as we reflect on Paul's lists of inappropriate behavior and fruit of the Spirit, but also corporately. How can a church together work at displaying these traits as a community? As we do that we must remember it is the work of the Spirit—God's work, not ours. Yet, just as we add compost and prune fruit trees to aid their production, we can together take actions to facilitate the Spirit's work in our midst.

Create alternative values. Writing in a strong honor culture, Paul did not attack the practice of honoring people and action, but rather advocated for an alternative set of values to honor. We must intentionally and openly do the same. David deSilva writes:

> We also need very much to increase our conversations with one another concerning what God does value and what values God hopes will direct his children—this is vital, since there is so much conversation happening about what is valuable to and valued by the secular society. When we do not speak out to one another, we by our silence collude with society's indoctrination of the values of pluralism, the privatization of religion, the importance of the bottom line, the eschatological idea of financial wealth, the promotion of consumerism to the point of a virtual return to debt slavery (deSilva 2000, 90-91).

Personal Response

- As you read over Paul's lists in verses 19-23 what are areas you sense the Spirit calling you to work on as an individual?

- What are actions you can take, composting and pruning, that can facilitate the Spirit's work in those areas?

- As you read over Paul's lists in verses 19-23 what are areas you sense the Spirit calling you to work on as a group or church?

- What are actions you can take together, composting and pruning, that can facilitate the Spirit's work in those areas?

- What shifts do you feel within you as read this section through the lens of an understanding of grace that includes reciprocity?

- How might living a more centered approach free your Christian fellowship to love more profoundly?

CHAPTER ELEVEN

Caring for Others in God's Family

The Text: Galatians 6:1-10

⁶ Brothers and sisters, if someone is caught in a sin, you who live by the Spirit should restore that person gently. But watch yourselves, or you also may be tempted. ² Carry each other's burdens, and in this way you will fulfill the law of Christ. ³ If anyone thinks they are something when they are not, they deceive themselves. ⁴ Each one should test their own actions. Then they can take pride in themselves alone, without comparing themselves to someone else, ⁵ for each one should carry their own load. ⁶ Nevertheless, the one who receives instruction in the word should share all good things with their instructor.

⁷ Do not be deceived: God cannot be mocked. A man reaps what he sows. ⁸ Whoever sows to please their flesh, from the flesh will reap destruction; whoever sows to please the Spirit, from the Spirit will reap eternal life. ⁹ Let us not become weary in doing good, for at the proper time we will reap a harvest if we do not give up. [10] *Therefore, as we have opportunity, let us do good to all people, especially to those who belong to the family of believers.*

The Flow and Form of the Text

Paul continues to focus on ethics in this section and as in the previous section his exhortation displays concern for the wellbeing of the community. As John Barclay observes, "Paul lived in a face-to-face society where self-advertisement, rivalry, and public competition were a perpetual cause of tension in everyday life" (Barclay 2014, 310). Paul here continues to present a vision of communal life profoundly different than the normal competition for status and honor.

The Text Explained

Centered church discipline (6:1). Paul is realistic. He recognizes that there will be sin. People will not always walk in the way of the Spirit (5:16-25). In this first verse he calls for what many would call "church discipline." For some that phrase will bring up negative images, and perhaps personal memories, of a bounded church confronting sin in way that leaves a person mired in shame. If that is the case for you, then you may accept that a centered church will give ethical direction about appropriate and inappropriate behavior as Paul did in the previous chapter, but you may resist what Paul points to in this verse—talking directly with someone about their sin. You may feel that would be bounded not centered. Yet, as in the example of centered soccer playing in chapter 9, there are situations in which a centered church must say, "No, we cannot accept that behavior in our community." A centered church has an inclusive character, but it is not universally inclusive.

Members of a bounded church get their status and security from the boundary line. Therefore, maintaining the clarity of the line and upholding the standard are high values for the group. When someone strays across the line and sins, the group's central concern is not the person but preserving the line of distinction that defines the group. That leads to the person on the wrong side of the line feeling shamed and excluded; and it reinforces the sense of superiority of those on the other side of the line. This is not to say that a bounded church would be totally unconcerned about the impact on the person or disinterested in restoration, but prioritizing the line twists the process in a hurtful direction. In the first century, the competitive honor-shame culture people looked for ways to put others down and lift themselves up—to score status points at the expense of others. The bounded religious approach reinforced the default practice in societal life.

Paul calls the Galatians to practice something radically different than the culture or the bounded ways of the other missionaries. Let us first look at two key words: "restore" and "gently." Paul does not outline specific steps, but he makes clear that the goal is restoration. The Greek word is the same as that used to describe the act of fisherman mending their nets (Mk 1:19). It has the sense of repairing and bringing something back to the way it was before. The primary object is not maintaining the standard, but of reorienting the person, restoring them to the path of walking in the way of Jesus Christ, and restoring them to the church fellowship. The probability of reaching the goal of restoration will increase if the process is characterized by gentleness.

As significant as the goal, is who is involved in the process. Paul writes "you who live by the Spirit." In Greek that is a plural "you." This is a communal action guided by the Spirit. It calls for praying and listening to the Spirit—discernment of a group of people on how to best respond in a gentle way that will lead to restoration.

In the second part of the verse Paul exhorts them to be careful lest they also be tempted (6:1). Two interpretations appear possible. Perhaps Paul had both in mind. It could be a caution about being tempted by the same sin as the person they are seeking to restore. A second possibility seems likely in the context of this letter, and specifically the preceding and following verses (5:26; 6:3-4). It could be a warning against feeling superior to the person who has sinned. That would be falling into distorting the gospel in a bounded line-drawing way as the other missionaries had done.

Mutual love (**6:2**). It is important that we interpret carrying burdens in relation to the previous verse *and* in the context of the whole letter. First, to walk with someone caught in sin with the goal of restoration is itself to help with their burden. Yet, sin often leads to other problems that people will need help with; and sin often arises from other burdens people carry. We are called to help others with symptoms and root problems.

Paul does not, however, write "help the sinner with their burdens" but "carry each other's burdens." He is pointing to more than just the specific situation in the first verse. We do well to relate this verse to others such as, "remember the poor" (2:10); "faith expressing itself through love" (5:6); "serve one another humbly in love" (5:13); "do good to all" (6:10). It is a call for the community as a whole to practice mutual support in a full range of actions rooted in love. Many of us live relatively stable lives and thus may tend to relate this verse to emotional, relational and spiritual burdens. We do appropriately include those when we read this text. Let us also remember that those receiving this letter in first-century-Roman-Empire Galatia lived more precariously economically, socially, physically, and politically than most of us. To be part of a family of faith that practiced mutual support would increase the circle of people with whom they would practice the lifestyle of mutually giving and receiving support. It was very concrete good news.

Reading this verse with the whole letter in mind adds depth in another way. The status-seeking systems of the "present evil age" (1:4), including the bounded religiosity of the agitators, make distinctions to put down others and raise up oneself or one's group. That produces envy, shame, division, judgmentalism, and even violence (1:13-14; 2:11-14; 5:15, 26). As we observed in chapter seven, at the cross Jesus did the exact opposite of that status seeking—both modeling a different approach and enabling the possibility of living a different reality (3:13, 28). As David Harvey observes, to be liberated from status-seeking line-drawing frees the community from the pressure of envy, competition, and conceitedness and frees them to focus on mutual love (Harvey 2016, 221). Thus, what Paul writes here about sharing each other's burdens is integrally related to the major themes of the letter and our ongoing discussion of bounded ways contrasted to centered ways.

It might surprise us that Paul here uses the word "law" positively after having used it so negatively in the letter. This reinforces the observation that Paul is not against law in a universal sense; he is critical of the law used as a tool of status-grabbing division as described in the previous paragraph. Scholars have put forward a variety of theories on what Paul means by "law of Christ." We cannot know for sure, but the text does enable us to make some general affirmations. First, based on Galatians 5:14 it is clear that Paul is not setting up a new law alternative to the law of Moses. Second, both by the words of carrying each other's burdens, and the link to Jesus Christ we can say that self-sacrificial love characterizes the law of Christ. Lastly, "law of Christ" refers not just to content but to its centered application in contrast to the bounded application of works of the law by the other missionaries.

Now, with all of this analysis of these first two verses in mind let's pause for a moment and sit with the Galatians as they hear these words. Rather than threats of exclusion for not measuring up to standards, they hear an emphasis on restoration. Rather than law being associated with those standards of status and exclusion, it is associated with caring for each other. Imagine them having a moment of realization that the focus is not on demonstrating worth, but as persons of worth they are called to love and be loved. What might the Galatians have thought and felt as the words of these two verses sank into their being?

Our actions do matter but stop playing comparison games (6:3-10). In these verses Paul again exhorts them to avoid the comparison with others that flows from line drawing (see also 1:10, 13; 5:26; 6:1b). Note that he affirms evaluating one's actions (6:4). The problem is doing so in a way that leads to feeling superior to others.

If I were Paul's editor, I would suggest that for the sake of clarity he use different language in verse five than he did in verse two. It is not as contradictory as it appears. The words are the same, but the context is different. In one he is talking about offering help, in the other he is making the point that each person is responsible for their actions. Both are true—pay attention to your own behavior and help others with their needs.

In one sense his next comment about supporting those who teach them can feel like a random side comment. It does, however, relate to the overall theme of mutual love, and even if in an implicit way, makes an important point. When Paul says that "each one should carry their own load" (6:5) he is not suggesting that followers of Jesus walk on their own. The fact that he talks about instructors demonstrates that he expects them to receive guidance from others.

In the final verses of this section (6:7-10) Paul summarizes main points of the larger unit (5:13-6:6). The works of the flesh (5:19-21) lead to destruction and judgment. The fruit of the Spirit (5:22-25; 6:9) leads to eternal life. The final verse, beginning with "therefore" brings together many threads from 5:13-6:6, "let us do good to all people, especially to those who belong to the family of believers" (6:10). If one reads these verses through the lens of a bounded church approach or through the lens of a modern Western concept of grace, it could appear that Paul here turns away from his message of grace and his centered approach. (For an explanation of these dynamics see the explanation of grace in chapter three and the implications section in the previous chapter.) Let us read with other lenses. What do we see?

First, rather than seeing these as conditional statements of acquiring status and belonging (if you do X then you earn this response), we can read them as descriptive statements. Those enmeshed in the present evil age, whose identity is in the status-seeking efforts of the world and who live according to its norms will live in ways that produce destruction. Those who, through the grace of God, are part of a community whose identity is in Jesus Christ and through the Spirit live according to the norms of the cross, will experience eternal life rather than destruction. Second, the metaphor he uses reinforces this descriptive reading. This is what happens. You *will* reap what you sow. (It is a common biblical image: Job 4:8; Psalm 126:5; Proverbs 22:8; Hosea 8:7; 1 Corinthians 9:11; 2 Corinthians 9:6.) Third, the image points to including human action as important, but not only human action. As in 5:16-26 (specifically 5:17) the flesh and Spirit are active forces. Like soil they have a role in what is produced ("from the flesh will reap . . ." "from the Spirit will reap . . .").

Through these alternative lenses, in the final verse we do not see doing good as an effort to be worthy of God's grace. Instead, it is both fitting response to God's grace and what flows from being in a community of others united with Christ and being led by the Spirit.

A final observation about this section and the previous one (Galatians 5:13-6:10): centered church ethics and bounded church ethics will both create distinctions from other groups and contribute to the group's identity. The difference is that in a bounded group the fundamental purpose of a to-do list is drawing a line that enables status measurement. That influences both the content of the list of imperatives and how they are used. Imagine neighbors in Galatia talking about one group and then the other: "That group acts so superior, if you don't follow their Jewish customs you can't even eat with them" vs. "That group is so welcoming, they would gladly let us eat with them, but honestly I'm not sure about eating with such a mixed group of people. The way they disregard status is unsettling. Yet, I feel attracted to them. They are so kind and giving to each other—and even people outside their group."

Significant Concept: Holistic Gospel

Living in Honduras led me to read the Bible with new eyes. My neighbors were extremely poor. They often lacked even the most basic necessities. In Honduras, the gap between the wealthy few and impoverished many was immense and the injustices that perpetuated the gap were obvious. Corruption and abuse of power were commonplace. I heard disturbing accounts of civilian massacres as war raged in neighboring countries. Biblical passages about justice and the poor stood out in a way they had not before.

My concept of what it meant to be a follower of Jesus broadened. I paid more attention to the theme of the Kingdom of God in the Bible. I shared more generously with my poor neighbors and looked for ways to address systemic causes of poverty and injustice. Yet no matter how passionately I would call other Christians to work to alleviate poverty and lessen injustice, no matter how many verses on these themes I would read to them, most still seemed to view acts to aid the impoverished and oppressed as good things to do, but not central. As Plutarco Bonilla observed, for many Christians social concern is like an appendix to the gospel; it could be removed without significant consequences (Bonilla 1987, 67). And, when I was most honest with myself, it did not feel central to me either. I pondered why it was that themes that are so prominent in the Bible, and ones that were concretely of such great importance for my neighbors, still felt like optional add-ons to the gospel. This drawing displays the answer I came to at that time.

The Kingdom of God and biblical themes of justice, liberating the oppressed, caring for the poor and marginalized, and healing the sick

The gospel—individual, spiritual salvation

For me the gospel was about forgiveness of sins and salvation for the individual. When I did evangelism that is how I explained it—salvation was freedom from guilt today and eternal life in heaven in the future. I recognized the topics in the bigger box as biblical and important, but the gospel was central; it was what was *most* important. I could not fit the bigger box into the smaller box. My concept of salvation did not have room for the themes on the left.

When I asked myself where I got the version of the gospel represented by the smaller box, the answer was: from Paul. I had memorized John 3:16 as a young child and grew up in churches that read the gospels with great interest, but our understanding of the gospel came from Paul. And the gospel, this Pauline version, was central. I lived with the tension of these two boxes for a number of years until Richard Hays led me to ask the questions I posed in the first chapter of this book. When I removed the lens of Luther's experience and read Paul anew, I saw that the Pauline gospel box was not as small as I had thought.

This section of the letter, combined with 2:10, displays that Paul was concerned about physical needs, not just spiritual. Yet to just state that could still leave us with the above two boxes. As discussed in the previous chapter, for many who read the letter through the lens of Luther's experience, this part of the letter is a sort of appendix. It is good and important material but not integrally related to the heart of the letter—the gospel. If, however, we read this section of the letter through the lenses we have used throughout this commentary, we end up with one box—a Pauline concept of the gospel that is holistic. I invite you to reflect on the variety of ways that is true. I will briefly point to just five important elements.

First, I have repeatedly drawn attention to the way Galatians 1:4, "rescue from the present evil age" and Galatians 6:15 "new creation," function as pillars in this letter. Neither has a future-salvation-only character. As Ryan Schellenberg states, "The good news is not just that we will keep on living in the present evil for the time being but now know we will get saved in the future. Rather the gospel is the good news of new creation that is already underway in transformed communities that blossom with the fruit of the Spirit. The present evil age is being destroyed. Yes, it will be completed in the future, but God is already bringing about new creation" (Schellenberg 2022).

Second, we have seen throughout the letter a concern for individuals and the community. To be justified, brought into right relationship with God, is also to be brought into relationship with others. One cannot separate the individual and the communal in the gospel. To recognize Paul's concern for the unity and wellbeing of the church community leads to giving importance not just to the individual, spiritual, and eternal future, but also to life in the present, the physical and interpersonal.

Third, Paul was not simply correcting a mistaken doctrinal teaching about works and salvation but confronting a lived out religious distortion of the gospel. This underscores that the letter is about lived out realities not an abstract statement of a doctrine.

Fourth, we have repeatedly seen the interrelatedness of various words, concepts, and parts of the letter. Although I, and others, had turned the "Pauline" gospel into a few propositions, the gospel proclaimed in Galatians cannot easily be disentangled and articulated in a few bullet points nor contained in one small box. It is rich, deep, broad—holistic.

Fifth, understanding grace as including an element of reciprocity, as explored in the previous chapter, leads to viewing the actions described in this section of the letter and the previous one as integral to the Pauline gospel of grace. Unlike the "Pauline" gospel that caused my two-box problem, the Pauline gospel we observe in Galatians is holistic.

To say that there is not actually a two-box problem is not to say we only keep one of the above boxes. Although it was impossible to fit all of the biblical themes from the larger box into the smaller box of the supposed Pauline gospel, there is no problem placing the biblical themes from the smaller box within the larger holistic gospel as displayed below. Note, even in this section of the letter there is talk of spiritual *and* physical, individual *and* communal, present *and* eternal. This is a very important point. Some simply use the term "holistic gospel" to justify focusing on the themes in the large box above and ignoring the smaller-box themes. A truly holistic gospel includes both.

Holistic gospel

The above diagram helps display the possibility of bringing the two together, but it also miscommunicates. Having a distinct box within the bigger boxes hides the interwovenness of the themes in Paul and the Bible.

Individual, spiritual, salvation is a facet of the holistic gospel that emanates throughout the whole.

If I could speak to my younger self I would say: the path to understanding concern for the oppressed and the poor as integral to a life of discipleship to Jesus is not to just turn up the volume on biblical texts like Luke 4:16-19 or Isaiah 58, but also to help Christians recognize the holistic nature of the gospel in Paul. After removing the barrier of the supposedly Pauline gospel that is only individual, spiritual, and future, other biblical texts will no longer feel like optional add-ons. Paul presents a gospel that is full, rich, and multilayered like what Jesus proclaims in the Gospels.

Implications of the Text for Today

Articulate the gospel in ways more authentic to Paul. In order to diminish the two-box problem described above, we need to broaden and deepen the language we use to explain the gospel. This is important in any teaching or conversation about the gospel, but especially in evangelism and interacting with seekers. Let us reflect carefully on what conceptual foundation we are laying for their Christian life. It is certainly appropriate to use words like repent, forgiveness, God's grace, and eternal life, but let us add words from themes observed in Galatians such as: adoption into God's family—including a sense of giving and receiving sibling love; freedom from shame and restoration of dignity; freedom from destructive powers; receiving and following the Holy Spirit; and a call to follow the way of Jesus. When we use the word "repent" let us portray it not just as a balancing of a legal ledger in heaven but as a turning from one way of life to a new center, and when we describe God's grace let us follow Paul in describing its radical inclusiveness in relation to worth and its sense of calling for a response. For example, we could describe grace in this way: "Through Jesus life, death, and resurrection God has opened the way for anyone, regardless of status, worth, or merit to be part of God's family and then God calls us to live in ways consistent with being members of that family." I do not mean to imply we need to say this whole list every time we articulate the gospel, nor to imply this is a complete list of all we could include. Rather I seek to point to different ways we can follow Paul in broadening our explanation of the gospel—broadening it beyond the supposed Pauline gospel of justification by faith understood narrowly.

Discipline is needed but must be done in a centered way. Discipline in bounded churches is often driven by a concern to maintain the line of distinction between appropriate and inappropriate behavior because that provides security; it defines who belongs. Too easily, the person being disciplined is not the ultimate concern and is hurt through the process. In response, many fuzzy churches rarely practice church discipline or even name some behaviors as sinful. That solves some problems but creates others. Not practicing what Paul calls for in 6:1 leaves people who are floundering, or hurting themselves and others, not receiving the direction they need. Rather than avoiding intervention, we must refurbish the reputation of church discipline through practicing it in a centered way. In a centered church, the purpose of discipline is to maintain the integrity of the relationship between the person and the center— Jesus Christ, and to maintain healthy relationships between those in the church community. In a bounded church the act of exposing and excluding the disciplined person itself fulfills the purpose. In a centered church the purpose is not met until the person is restored. Thinking of the diagram in chapter one, if the person's arrow has changed direction and they have turned their back on the center, it is appropriate to recognize they are no longer in relationship with the center. But the goal is to help them change direction. We must practice what Paul calls for in 6:1 and in the way he describes. It does not matter whether you call it church discipline, loving intervention, confrontation, or something else, what matters is that we work to redeem this practice so that people will think of it as part of loving someone into being more the person God created them to be. Let us practice it in ways that will feel like a gift rather than a curse.

Church discipline requires mutual commitment. Note that Paul's exhortation to practice restorative discipline is within a section that emphasizes mutual care within a church community (6:1-2, 10) and within a letter in which Christian community is a major theme. The two go together, as Dallas Nord observed in a class discussion, "Before Paul's restorative discipline can be attempted, there must be a mutual commitment of individuals to the community, and the community to each individual."

Church discipline requires discernment. Scott Carolan says that before any intervention, he has a conversation with other church staff or lay leaders. He asks, "Help me think through this, how do we handle this in a centered way?" A key question they ask is, "What is most loving for this person?" (Baker 2021, 160–61). Importantly a key part of the discernment is listening to the person themselves and seeking to understand the situation. As I imagine those led by the Spirit, in Galatia or today putting in practice what Paul calls for, I picture a group of people gathered to pray, discern, and ask questions like: How do we respond to this situation? What is best for the person and the community? What will lead to restoration? What do they need? How can we express our love throughout the process? Who are people who would be best able to communicate with them?

For numerous examples of churches doing what Paul calls for, gentle loving intervention with the goal of restoration, see chapters eight and nine in my book, Centered-Set Church: Discipleship and Community Without Judgmentalism.

Centered exhortation. In the implications section of the previous chapter we observed that Paul did not consider it problematic to have expectations of changed behavior nor to state examples of appropriate and inappropriate behavior and character traits. The problem was linking behavior and status. There are other significant differences between the ethical exhortations of a bounded group and Paul's centered approach. Think about the behaviors that the other missionaries emphasized and their purpose: they used circumcision, sabbath observance, and food laws as a clear line that defined those with insider status from outsiders. What were the behaviors that Paul emphasized in 5:13-6:10? What was their purpose? His centered approach freed him from line drawing. Rather than focusing on actions easy to measure and achieve, he focused on actions that would enhance the well-being of the individuals and the group as a whole. However, it is not just that stepping away from a bounded approach enabled Paul to focus on virtues and behaviors not so easily accomplished. His lists and imperatives impede people's natural tendency to draw bounded group lines. Although a few of the things Paul states could be easily measured (for instance, you get drunk or you do not), most are harder to clearly define as avoided or accomplished. Avoiding envy and selfish ambition, practicing kindness and gentleness, carrying each other's burdens and doing good to others do not lend themselves for use in bounded group line-drawing.

Let us follow Paul and not shy away from ethical exhortation. Let us follow Paul in throwing sand in the gears of the bounded approach by giving imperatives that are not easily measured. Let us follow Paul in calling others to actions and virtues that enhance the well-being of individuals and the church community.

Centered exhortation—indicative before imperative. The human religious inclination is to think we must do things to gain favor from God. Therefore, people, especially those who have experienced a bounded church, easily interpret ethical imperatives in bounded religious way. Whether in conversation, in a Bible study, or a sermon, rather than just stating a list of dos and don'ts, we should follow Paul's example. He both writes indicative material about God's gracious initiative before his ethical exhortation, and he writes more indicative content than imperatives. Reminding people that God's gracious action precedes our action and that we do not have to demonstrate worth in order receive God's gracious gift will help them not hear ethical exhortation in a bounded religious way.

For a more in-depth exploration of a centered exhortation, including examples of imperatives flowing from indicative statements, see chapter six in my book, *Centered-Set Church: Discipleship and Community Without Judgmentalism.*

Personal Response

- First, think of a time when someone confronted you in a way that was harsh. They scolded and shamed you, left you feeling inferior. Next, think of a time when someone gently, but clearly, confronted you by telling you that you were off-track, hurting yourself and others. It may still have been a difficult conversation for you, but it left you feeling loved, accompanied. Take some time and reflect on how different the two experiences felt. List things that made them different. What can you learn from the differences that will help you live out what Paul calls us to do in 6:1?

- Is it a bigger challenge for you to be less bounded or less fuzzy? How does that influence the way you think and feel as you read this section? What from this chapter in the commentary can help you become more centered?

- What are ways this chapter, and the essay on holistic gospel, have helped you see more similarities between Paul and Jesus?

- What shifts do you feel within yourself as read this section through the lens of an understanding of grace that includes reciprocity?

- Take a moment and listen to God's Spirit. Is God calling you to help someone else with a burden they are carrying (6:2)?

CHAPTER TWELVE

New Creation
Through the Cross

The Text: Galatians 6:11-18

¹¹ *See what large letters I use as I write to you with my own hand!*

¹² *Those who want to impress people by means of the flesh are trying to compel you to be circumcised. The only reason they do this is to avoid being persecuted for the cross of Christ.* ¹³ *Not even those who are circumcised keep the law, yet they want you to be circumcised that they may boast about your circumcision in the flesh.* ¹⁴ *May I never boast except in the cross of our Lord Jesus Christ, through which*[a] *the world has been crucified to me, and I to the world.* ¹⁵ *Neither circumcision nor uncircumcision means anything; what counts is the new creation.* ¹⁶ *Peace and mercy to all who follow this rule—to*[b] *the Israel of God.*

¹⁷ *From now on, let no one cause me trouble, for I bear on my body the marks of Jesus.*

¹⁸ *The grace of our Lord Jesus Christ be with your spirit, brothers and sisters. Amen.*

---

a. Galatians 6:14 Or *whom*
b. Galatians 6:16 Or *rule and to*

The Flow and Form of the Text

Paul himself writes this conclusion to the letter. It was a common practice at that time to dictate letters to a scribe (see Romans 16:22), and also common for the one dictating the letter to, with their own hand, write a short greeting or summary at the end of a letter. It served as a stamp of authenticity and added a personal touch. It would be like someone today adding a handwritten note to the bottom of a computer-generated letter. That is not to say these verses are a mere formality. Paul reviews principle points from the letter in condensed form with bold frankness.

Paul writes the words "circumcision" or "uncircumcision" six times in these few verses, eight if we include "flesh" which he probably uses with double meaning—referring to circumcision and the sinful force of the present evil age (see discussion of 5:16-17 in chapter ten). This confirms that circumcision was a key aspect of the conflict in Galatia. At the same time this section makes clear that although circumcision may have been the central point of disagreement, Paul does not view circumcision itself as the key issue. Note that he does not make an argument about circumcision itself, nor offer a counter proposal. He does not say "rather than circumcision the appropriate marker of distinction to demonstrate worth is _____." He makes explicitly clear he is not advocating for uncircumcision as the "right" thing and circumcision as "wrong" (6:15). This section, and thus the letter, is not a critique of circumcision but a critique of using circumcision as a religious boundary line, using it as a way of gaining status and avoiding shame.

As described in chapter one of this commentary, honor was highly valued and it was approached in a competitive way. For one person or group to gain honor another one lost honor. David

Harvey points out that in the common contested ways of that honor culture, the normal thing for Paul to do in response to the agitators seeking to gain honor at his expense would be to defend his honor. Instead in this section, Paul "objects to the whole process of status seeking" (Harvey 2016, 149).

The Text Explained

Selfish status grasping (6:12-13). Paul begins by arguing that circumcision itself is not the prime concern of the agitators; it is the social implications for them of the Galatian Christians being circumcised or not. In essence he is saying, "The other missionaries may act as if they are concerned for you, but in reality selfish concerns motivate them." Reading these verses through the lenses of a bounded-church approach and honor-shame dynamics add depth to our understanding. For instance, the phrase "impress people" appears clear enough, but through the lens of their honor-shame culture the Greek word translated as "impress people" also has the sense of saving face. They want to protect their honor. This helps us understand Paul's comment about avoiding persecution. He is not adding a new thought: point one, they want to impress people, point two, they want to avoid persecution. Rather, these two are joined. They want to save face and thus avoid persecution.

How is it that the Gentile believers getting circumcised and adhering to other Jewish practices would help these Jewish-Christian missionaries avoid persecution? Let us set aside the images we might have of contemporary use of the word "persecution"—of Christians suffering violence or imprisonment. In the context of gaining or maintaining honor, what might Paul have had in mind? First, a reminder that in their collectivist society the reputation of the group was preeminent. My tendency is to think, "what will they think of me?" in Paul's time the question was "what will they think of our group?" In a setting where people respected the old more than the new, and where religions had many rites and celebrations, it is likely that people insulted Christians. They participated in a new movement lacking recognition as an ancient religion, and rather than temples or established religious buildings, they met in people's homes. In contrast the Jewish religion was ancient, replete with celebrations and traditions, and met in synagogues. To identify with the Jewish religion would help Christians gain acceptance in society.

Even more significant for the agitators would be their concern for what Jews thought of them. It is likely that other Jews criticized Jewish Christians for joining together with Gentiles for their times of fellowship and prayer—even eating with them (cf. Acts 11:3). If the Gentile Christians adopted Jewish ways it would help the agitators save face and escape shaming ridicule (persecution) by neighbors of other religions and especially by other Jews.

In order to get the depth of meaning in verses 13 and 14, it is valuable to highlight the different attitude toward boasting then and in our context today. For us the English term refers to a socially unacceptable negative act of excessive pride. David Harvey points out that when Paul wrote, the word still carried the sense of public self-aggrandizement, but there were two key differences. First, it was a socially acceptable way to highlight difference or superiority. To boast was to make a claim for honor. Think of it like a group of children coming to adults and proudly saying, "Look what we did!" They are seeking affirmation. Similarly, in Paul's time boasts were submitted to the court of public opinion. If they were accepted, the boasting individual or group gained honor and standing above others. Second, boasting also impacted those listening. It had a formational role through defining what was honorable. Returning to the example of children, suppose you were a child playing with a separate group but you observed the positive response the other children received. You would then know that what they did is something that would gain praise. The positive response to the boasting of one group guided others to know what was honorable behavior. This relates to an important aspect about honor and shame that was stated in chapter one. The definition of what was honorable was not set, it varied in different groups and it could be modified. Boasting was one tool in reconfiguring a group's concept of honor (Harvey 2016, 93–97).

Thus, Paul's critique of the other missionaries' seeking to be able to boast about the Gentile Christians getting circumcised is a continuation of what he wrote in verse 12. Saving face, avoiding persecution, and boasting are each about honor and social consequences for the agitators. Looking at their boasting through the lens of a bounded approach adds depth to what is defined above and enables us to better understand how the Gentiles getting circumcised is something the other missionaries could boast about.

When someone outside of a bounded group changes their actions or beliefs in order to be on the right side of the line and join the group, the line is validated. When someone meets the requirements of a bounded group it reaffirms not just the importance of the line, but the status of the group itself. Someone wanting to be part of the group communicates that the group has value. Group members who persuade others to comply with the line and join the group will gain status. Therefore, if the Galatians submit and become circumcised the other missionaries could boast of their success. It would give the agitators higher status with other bounded group Jewish Christians, and the Galatians compliance would lend more credibility to the other missionaries' argument—communicating to other Gentile Christians, "This is the right thing to do."

To summarize, in these two verses Paul is warning the Galatians that the other missionaries are not concerned first and foremost about the Galatians. Rather, the agitators' fundamental concerns are saving face, avoiding shame, gaining honor, and reinforcing the security of their group through maintenance of their line. It is not, however, just a question of selfish motivations. In the next two verses Paul presses deeper to proclaim that the bounded group status-grasping of the other missionaries is in direct conflict with the way of Jesus Christ.

Boasting in the cross (6:14). We might give little importance to Paul's use of "boast"—thinking it is just an artful literary move to connect and contrast with the previous sentence. The English definition of boasting being a negative action might even propel us to move on rather than getting bogged down in trying to understand how it is okay to boast in this one way. Instead, let us keep in mind the alternative definition above and take seriously Paul's use of the word. He is making a statement about his honor status that will invite others to embrace the same definition of honor.

To put the word "boast" in its first century context, however, immediately brings up the incongruity of linking it with a cross. In the Roman world if one had any association with a crucified one the common action would be to hide or deny the connection, not boast about it. Many today, understandably, emphasize the physical torment of crucifixion, but in the first century it was the shame of crucifixion that was most feared. The fact that crosses, including Jesus', were placed near very public roads underscores the shaming intent. It was a public spectacle designed to degrade.

Why then does Paul make this oxymoronic statement about boasting in the cross? If we think of the cross just in terms of forgiveness of sins and individual salvation, it might be hard to explain. But in Galatians the cross is that and more, it is also the means "of a value-neutralizing social revolution" (Harvey 2016, 227) (1:4; 2;16; 3:13; 3:27-28). At the cross Jesus did the exact opposite of what Paul has accused the agitators of doing in the previous two verses. Rather than grasping for honor for himself, he repeatedly risked his reputation in order to express loving acceptance to the shamed and excluded—to the point of death on a shameful cross. His death exposed the honor systems of the day as distorted from the ways of God. The cross and resurrection not only exposed these systems but turned them on their head and provided freedom from them (1:4; Colossians 2:15). Through the resurrection God validated the way of Jesus as the truly honorable way. With this broader meaning of the cross in mind we can understand "the phrase 'boast in the cross' as an attempt to define Christ's shameful crucifixion as a paradigm for honourable behaviour for the Galatian Christians" (Harvey 2016, 181). Within the new honor system formed by the cross of Christ, Paul's statement is not paradoxical. Shame is relative to a group's definition of honor. The paradox is not within Paul's boasting in the cross, it is that the other missionaries are still seeking status in categories of differentiation dissolved by Christ's death.

When we allow "boasting" to have the sense of staking an honor claim and including an element of instruction about what is honorable, we can see that in the few words of this verse Paul is communicating key elements of this letter. Through Christ he, and the Galatians too, can be free from the bounded-group-status-grasping way of the world and embrace a radically different concept of honor. And it truly is radical. Paul is boasting, staking his identity, in the cross, something that undermines status differences. I invite you to pause for a moment and reflect on what that implies about a centered approach. It points to it not just being a retooling of bounded or fuzzy, it is a radically different third way. There is still honor, still a group sense of identity, of belonging, but it is of a totally different character—the bounded group's honor system turned upside down.

It is upside down because at its foundation a centered group is about God acting, not human actions. It is not about Paul, his ethnic group, his religious tradition. It is about God's gracious action and trusting in that saving action (2:16) enough to live according to this way instead of the world's status systems. But it is not just about Paul, or any other individual; Paul calls it a new creation.

Significant Concept: New Creation

The Pauline phrase "new creation" is well known. It is much more common, however, to hear people quote his use of the phrase in 2 Corinthians 5:17, than in Galatians 6:15 ("Neither circumcision nor uncircumcision means anything; what counts is the new creation" 6:15.) Although most translations of 6:15 do not explicitly interpret "new creation" as referring to an individual, many readers may hear the words as the equivalent of "new person" because they bring that meaning with them from 2 Corinthians. We can affirm that as an appropriate interpretative step—using one Pauline text to help interpret another one. But in this case we must first take a closer look at 2 Corinthians 5:17. Does that verse actually equate new creation with an individual person?

Following the lead of the King James Version, many translations do state that Paul is referring an individual person.

> Therefore, if anyone is in Christ, he is a new creation. The old has passed away; behold, the new has come (ESV).

> Anyone who belongs to Christ is a new person. The past is forgotten, and everything is new (CEV).

Reading translations like these, Christians generally interpret the verse as explaining what happens when a person experiences salvation. The saved person is a "new creation" who acts differently. They have left behind their old behavior and now practice a new morality. This translation and interpretation are not necessarily the most obvious or the best. The New American Standard Bible makes the subjectivity of the translation clearer by putting in italics the words that are not in the Greek original. "Therefore if anyone is in Christ, *this person is* a new creation; the old things passed away; behold, new things have come." For the sentence to flow and make sense in English some words, including a verb, must be put into the sentence where there are none in Greek. The original does not identify the new creation as a person; that is an interpretative move. The following two translations are just as appropriate.

> Therefore, if anyone is in Christ, the new creation has come: The old has gone, the new is here! (NIV).

> So if anyone is in Christ, there is a new creation: everything old has passed away; see, everything has become new! (NRSV).

In the Greek, 2 Corinthians 5:17 and Galatians 6:15 are much closer than they appear in English. The ESV translation comes close to a literal Greek translation of 6:15: "For neither circumcision counts for anything, nor uncircumcision, but a new creation."

Let us review what we have learned. Neither in 2 Corinthians 5:17 nor in Galatians 6:15 does Paul explicitly identify the new creation as an individual Christian. Versions of the Bible that do equate new creation with an individual are interpreting what they think Paul meant, but not translating actual words he wrote. Therefore, 2 Corinthians 5:17 does not actually provide extra insight on how to interpret Galatians 6:15. In Greek they are quite similar—both simply state "new creation" without description of what those words refer to.

Before giving my opinion on how to interpret this phrase I will offer some observations on why it matters. The there-is-a-new-person interpretation leads the reader to think of transformation of the individual and look inward. The there-is-a-new-creation interpretation leads the reader to look out and conceive of Christ's work in a broad way. The broader, or less individualistic, interpretation does not rule out significant changes occurring in individuals' lives, and it points to much more. The there-is-a-new-person reading, however, does rule out broader implications and limits the impact of the gospel to the individual.

For three reasons I think we do best to interpret "new creation" in a broader sense that includes transformation within and also a sense that the world has changed for those in Christ. First, it is a more restrained, less speculative translation. It does not add interpretative words.

Second, in a setting much more individualistic than Paul's we should be extra cautious of a translation that adds an individualistic emphasis that was not in the original. Recognizing that our default is to interpret things individualistically calls for us to be on guard for imposing that on the text.

Finally, the context of this verse in Galatians, both the immediate context and especially the letter as a whole, points to the broader interpretation. Paul has just made a statement that includes a sense of change in him and his world (6:14), and in the first lines of the letter (1:4) he writes about the cross dealing with personal sins and changing lived reality (rescue from the present evil age). To speak of rescue from the present evil age points to the world-changing, or cosmic, impact of the cross and resurrection. This points to Paul's already-but-not-yet view of the new age. He does not write of release from the present evil age as being a future-only liberation. It has happened in the present. This language at the beginning of the letter calls us to see "new creation" as a similar cosmic change which is unfolding now. Between those two points in the letter, there are numerous references to individual transformation and to a community of believers living in ways radically different than the world because of the work of Christ and the presence of the Spirit. The united table at Antioch is a concrete example of new creation that includes transformed individuals living according to new realities which are manifest in corporate actions. In Galatians, new creation is best interpreted as both individual and broader, not just one or the other.

—

What matters (6:15). For those shaped by bounded group religiosity, imagine how confusing, even shocking, these words must have been: "Neither circumcision nor uncircumcision means anything" (6:15). In a bounded-church mindset anything of importance gets pulled into line-drawing. When observing someone arguing so strongly against circumcision, a bounded-mentality person would naturally assume that stance against circumcision functions as a line. They would think, "if I want to measure up and be in that person's group I need to be against circumcision." So for Paul to say neither matters is baffling. But Paul is not fuzzy, this is not whateverism. He does not say with an indifferent shrug, "circumcision, uncircumcision, whatever." There is something that matters, it is new creation. Again, as in the previous verses in this section, the issue is not circumcision itself. In terms of this commentary, in this verse Paul is saying, bounded-church lines, whatever their content, are not important, what matters is living out an in-Christ, centered approach. God's action through Jesus Christ has freed the Galatians from the former and provides the possibility of living together in a totally new way.

Similarly, from the perspective of the honor system of the day to say this marker of distinction and identity does not matter is not just confusing, but unsettling. David Harvey observes, "Difference was the basis of any claim to honour, 'for if everyone attains equal honour then there is no honour for anyone.' The hubris common amongst ancient groups was expressly focused on accentuating difference. . . . Whereas the present age is defined by differentiation, Paul's new creation is a place where the value of the evil age's binary divisions have been removed" (Harvey 2016, 153, 163). They do not matter. What matters is in fact the opposite. In God's new creation what matters is to *not* grasp for status based on differentiation, what matters is to *not* shame others as inferior because of their ethnicity or social status. What *does* matter is being in Christ in a church community that does not make distinctions between Greek or Jew, slave or free, male or female, and where all seek the welfare of the others in the church.

This is the last sentence in the body of the letter before Paul's closing words of blessing. It as if he is saying, "If I you have not already understood, let me make this clear, what counts is not whether you are following one set of rules and distinctions or another, what counts is whether you are rooted in the present evil age or in the new reality created by the cross." Take note what he does not say. He does not say, "If you have not already understood, let me make this clear, it is incorrect to teach that salvation is by works, the correct teaching is salvation by grace." The sentence is correct, this teaching is part of new creation reality. But it alone does not come close to having the depth, breadth, or richness of what Paul actually said, nor of capturing the actual problems in Galatia. For this reason, Paul began the letter by writing about freedom from the present evil age and he ends with words of new creation.

Final words, peace, mercy, grace (6:16-18). Paul has pronounced curses on those who have distorted the gospel. He ends the letter with words of blessing. They are traditional Hebraic words of blessing, peace, and mercy, corresponding to *shalom* and *hesed*. He pronounces this blessing on those who follow, or walk according to, the way of the cross and new creation he has just described. Once again, he directly challenges the agitators' definition of God's people—the Israel of God are new creation people.

After words of blessing for those who follow the way of the cross, Paul appeals to the agitators to stop causing problems. He bases his appeal on bearing on his body the marks of Jesus. He is likely referring to actual physical scars from beatings (2 Corinthians 4:8-10). But he probably meant more than that. The Greek word he used is the same word used for the marks that masters branded on the skin of slaves with a hot iron, and for religious tattoos. Ryan Schellenberg observes, "Paul seems to draw a metaphorical connection between the marks of his suffering and tattoos worn to indicate the god or master to whom one belonged" (Schellenberg 2003, 21). So, the appeal for the other missionaries to stop attacking him is based on his having demonstrated his commitment to the gospel and because of who his master is—Jesus.

Paul ends this passionate letter containing many strong words of confrontation, with words of blessings that affirm their brotherly and sisterly relationship. He begins and ends the letter with words of grace (1:3-4; 6:16, 18), and, even when the word is not used, the grace of God permeates the letter. It is the foundation of the letter. Paul likely writes the final word, "amen"—may it be so—with passion and hope. Praying that those listening to the letter will responding affirmatively to the letter and join him in saying, "Amen."

Implications of the Text for Today

Be aware of our line-drawing tendencies. Paul describes the other missionaries in such starkly negative terms it is easy to label them as villains—very different than us. Remember that they were followers of Jesus, missionary teachers who left their homes with the intent of helping the cause of Christ. I say this not to soften Paul's critique of their bounded-church distortion of the gospel, but to keep us from thinking of them as so different from us. Instead, let us look for ways we might have similarities with the other missionaries. Today, as then, people gain status through comparison, raise their group up by putting others down, and adjust their behavior to gain praise or avoid shame. This section of Galatians calls us to be aware of these tendencies, to recognize that society's definitions of honor and status are often twisted. It is a word of warning that good intentions are not enough to protect us from the destructive effects of line-drawing judgmentalism.

There is an alternative. Even more important than the "no" in this section, stated in the previous paragraph, is the "yes." The cross of Jesus opens up a radically different alternative to these status games. We do not have to put others down or live up to twisted standards of success and status in order to have a sense of value and identity. Through the cross, Jesus exposed and tore down one system and replaced it with another. Let us live according to the honorable ways defined by the cross.

New creation through cruciform means. God exercised power and brought change through the cross. A new creation vision is compelling, and we can be tempted to work at it through creating godly rules and enforcing them. The cross displays an alternative way, a non-coercive power. A centered approach is cruciform in two ways. First, it is grounded in God's action—what God did through the cross. Second, the cross serves as an example, as described above. Jesus' actions on the cross were the opposite of the status-grasping ways of bounded group religiosity.

Broader concept of new creation. Individual salvation, individual morality, and individual transformation all matter, yet an overly individual reading of the Bible can limit our awareness of the broader and deeper work that God has done. It can limit our imagination for what God can do in our midst today. Let us portray new creation as something that includes God's work within individuals, but also as much more than that.

Personal Response

- What are different ways status is measured, gained, and lost in the society you live in today? What are the implications for you of taking seriously Paul's proclamation that these distinctions have been dissolved by the cross?

- What does Jesus' honor code look like today? What types of behaviors/attitudes are worthy of boasting about within the upside-down honor code?

- If Paul were writing this letter to confront bounded tendencies in your church what are things he might say instead of circumcision and uncircumcision? "Neither _____ nor _____ means anything; what counts is the new creation."

- What are new creation realities you have experienced or observed?

May things you have learned and reflected on through reading Galatians and this book contribute to you and your faith community experiencing more of new creation reality through the working of God's Spirit.

Acknowledgements

As I recounted in the introduction to this book, reading an essay on Galatians by Richard Hays led me into a new way of interpreting Galatians and excited me with the transformative potential of that interpretation. That was the seed of this book. But I am indebted to Richard for so much more than that essay. I had the opportunity to study Galatians with Richard while working on my PhD in theology. With that input alone Richard would have been a key shaping influence of my interpretation of Galatians. But it is my good fortune that Richard later wrote a commentary on Galatians that added further insights and was a great aid in writing this book. It has been a privilege to walk in Richard's shadow, and I am deeply grateful for the many ways he has contributed to this work.

Although I have a master's degree in New Testament, and I took a couple doctoral level courses in New Testament studies, I am a theologian, not a Bible scholar. Yet in a surprising way, since my days of doctoral study through to the present some of my closest friends have been Pauline scholars. They have done three things for me. They have filled in some of the holes and gaps in my knowledge of Paul and his writings. They have been my teachers. This work is better because of what I have learned from them. Second, their excitement about Paul's writing and its message for the church today has fed my own. Third, in each case we were first and foremost friends. Talks about Paul's letters have been part of the friendship, but there is so much more. I have been nourished by these relationships. Out of gratitude I dedicate this book to them, in chronological order of when we first met: Audrey West, Ross Wagner, Jon Isaak, Ryan Schellenberg, Andy Johnson, and Amy Whisenand Krall.

The input of Richard Hays, my Pauline scholar friends, and other Bible scholars quoted in this book is significant, but I would not have been able to utilize it if it had not been for Joel Green. He persuaded me that rather than getting a master's degree in theology, I should get a master's degree in New Testament before continuing studies in theology. Without that foundation and the tools I received from Joel I would not have been able to write this commentary.

It has not just been interaction with books and scholarly friends that has shaped this commentary. I have tested ideas in classes and seminars and learned from my students. I am particularly grateful to the people of Amor Fe y Vida Church in Tegucigalpa, Honduras and students in Galatians courses I have taught at Fresno Pacific Biblical Seminary (formerly Mennonite Brethren Biblical Seminary) and once in Bogota at Seminaro Biblico Menonita de Colombia.

It is one thing to have the ideas and information mentioned in the previous paragraphs, it is another thing to write a book about them. Without Raymond Bystrom I doubt you would be holding this book in your hands right now. I committed to doing this book many years ago, and more than once had assumed the Luminaire series had died and I had missed my chance. At other times I was not sure I wanted to do the work of writing the book. Ray has done much to keep the series alive and, particularly, at a few key moments encouraged me to move ahead with the project. I am grateful for his encouragement (and patience!).

I had the unusual idea of not starting this commentary in the usual way, with chapter one, verse, one, but with the story in Antioch from chapter two. Feeling insecure about the idea I felt the need for support from a Bible scholar. While canoeing on a small lake on the Indiana-Michigan border I asked Ryan Schellenberg's opinion of my idea. Ryan not only gave me the "permission" I was seeking, he helped me think about how to do it. Ryan later agreed to read the manuscript. As mentioned above, he knows a lot more about Paul than I do, and he saved me from a number of errors and weak arguments. I would have been grateful for that, but what thrilled me about Ryan's input is that every time he challenged me to change something he also helped me see how that change would not just be more "correct" but would make my argument stronger. It is quite common in acknowledgments, after a comment like this, to say something like, "but any errors are my own." That has always felt like something one is supposed to say. But now I understand and want to say it. This book is much better because of all of the input Ryan gave, the shortcomings that remain are mine, not his.

After I worked through the manuscript, making changes in response to Ryan's input, I asked five other people to read it. I am grateful for the insights they offered, for pointing out places that were unclear, for suggesting additional response questions, and correcting errors. You the reader can be very grateful for this unselfish labor by Lynn Baker, Garry Bortz, Ken Esau, Dallas Nord, and Jessica Rutkosky.

I also want to thank those who read and gave feedback on portions of the manuscript: David Cramer, Ana Magana, Connie Nicholson, Jamie Pitts, John Roth, and Luis Tapia.

It is a privilege to have worked with Dora Dueck an editor I trust and respect. I am grateful for her suggestions and for her catching errors I had missed. Numerous sentences are clearer and easier to read because of her work. Thanks to Carson Samson of Kindred Productions for shepherding this manuscript through the production process. I especially appreciated his openness to process together various questions that came up along the way.

As with all my books, I am deeply grateful to my wife Lynn for the many ways she has supported and helped me as I wrote this book.

Finally, my gratitude to the Apostle Paul for writing this letter that continues to move and challenge me even after so many years of studying it. And ultimately my deepest appreciation and gratitude is to the one who Paul calls us to center on—Jesus Christ.

References

Arens, Eduardo. 2009. *Han Sido Llamados a La Libertad: La Carta de San Pablo a Los Gálatas y Su Actualidad*. Lima: Centro de Estudios y Publicaciones.

Baker, Marcos. 2014. *Gálatas*. Comentario Biblico Iberoamericano. Buenos Aires: Ediciones Kairos.

Baker, Mark D. 1990. "Responding to the Powers: Learning From Paul and Jesus." Master's Thesis, Berkeley, CA: New College for Advanced Christian Studies/GTU.

———. 1999. *Religious No More: Building Communities of Grace & Freedom*. Downers Grove, IL: InterVarsity Press.

———. 2021. *Centered-Set Church: Discipleship and Community Without Judgmentalism*. Downers Grove, IL: IVP Academic.

Barclay, John M. G. 1988. *Obeying the Truth: A Study of Paul's Ethics in Galatians*. Edinburgh: T&T Clark.

———. 2014. "Grace and the Countercultural Reckoning of Worth." In *Galatians and Christian Theology: Justification, the Gospel, and Ethics in Paul's Letter*, edited by Mark W. Elliot, Scott J. Hafemann, and John Frederick. Grand Rapids, MI: Baker Academic.

———. 2015. *Paul and the Gift*. Grand Rapids, MI: Eerdmans.

———. 2016. "The Meaning of God's Grace." *HonorShame* (blog). January 20, 2016. http://honorshame.com/the-meaning-of-gods-grace/.

———. 2020. *Paul and the Power of Grace*. Grand Rapids, MI: Eerdmans.

Barclay, John M. G., and Wesley Hill. 2016. "The Scandalous Gift of Grace." *Christianity Today*, January 2016.

Boersma, Hans. 2004. *Violence, Hospitality, and the Cross: Reappropriating the Atonement Tradition*. Grand Rapids, MI: Baker Academic.

Bonilla, Plutarco. 1987. "Crisis Del Protestantismo Costarricense Actual." *Pastoralia* 9 (July): 65–128.

Bruce, F. F. 1982. *The Epistle to the Galatians: A Commentary on the Greek Text*. The New International Greek Testament Commentary. Grand Rapids, MI: Eerdmans.

deSilva, David A. 2000. *Honor, Patronage, Kinship & Purity: Unlocking New Testament Culture*. 1st Edition. Downers Grove, IL: IVP Academic.

Dunn, James D. G. 2008. *The New Perspective on Paul*. Second Edition, Revised. Grand Rapid, MI: Eerdmans Publishing.

Ellul, Jacques. 1983. *Living Faith: Belief and Doubt in a Perilous World*. San Francisco: Harper & Row.

Gaventa, Beverly Roberts. 2000. "Is Galatians Just A 'Guy Thing'?: A Theological Reflection." *Interpretation: A Journal of Bible and Theology* 54 (3): 267–78.

Gorman, Michael J. 2013. "Paul and the Cruciform Way of God in Christ." *Journal of Moral Theology* 2 (1): 64–83.

———. 2019. *Participating in Christ: Explorations in Paul's Theology and Spirituality*. Grand Rapids, MI: Baker Academic.

Harvey, David S. 2016. "Face in Galatians: 'Boasting in the Cross' as Reconfigured Honour in Paul's Letter." Ph. D. Thesis, University of Manchester.

Hays, Richard B. 1986. "Jesus' Faith and Ours: A Rereading of Galatians 3." In *Conflict and Context: Hermeneutics in the Americas*, edited by Mark Lau Branson and C. René Padilla, 274–80. Grand Rapids, MI: Eerdmans.

———. 1992. "Justification." In *Anchor Bible Dictionary*, edited by David

N. Freedman, III:1129–33. New York: Doubleday.

———. 1999. "The Conversion of the Imagination: Scripture and Eschatology in 1 Corinthians." *New Testament Studies* 45 (3): 391–412. https://doi.org/10.1017/S0028688598003919.

———. 2000. "The Letter to the Galatians." In *The New Interpreter's Bible*, 11:181–348. Nashville: Abingdon Press.

———. 2008. "What Is 'Real Participation in Christ'?: A Dalogue with E. P. Sanders on Pauline Soteriology." In *Redefining First-Century Jewish and Christian Identities: Essays in Honor of Ed Parish Sanders*, edited by Fabian Udoh, 336–51. Norte Dame, IN: University of Notre Dame Press.

———. 2014. "Apocalyptic Poiēsis in Galatians: Paternity, Passion, and Participation." In *Galatians and Christian Theology: Justification, the Gospel, and Ethics in Paul's Letter*, edited by Mark W. Elliot, Scott J. Hafemann, N T. Wright, and John Frederick, 200–219. Grand Rapids, MI: Baker Academic.

Hiebert, Paul G. 1978. "Conversion, Culture and Cognitive Categories." *Gospel in Context* 1 (4): 24–29.

———. 1994. *Anthropological Reflections on Missiological Issues*. Grand Rapids, MI: Baker Academic.

Larsen, Timothy. 2020. "George MacDonald and Victorian Earnestness about Faith and Anxieties about Doubt." *Mars Hill Audio* 148.

Lendon, J. E. 1997. *Empire of Honour: The Art of Government in the Roman World*. 1st edition. Oxford : New York: Clarendon Press.

Longenecker, Bruce W. 2010. *Remember the Poor: Paul, Poverty, and the Greco-Roman World*. Grand Rapids, MI: Eerdmans Publishing.

Martyn, J. Louis, ed. 1997. *Galatians: A New Translation with Introduction and Commentary*. 1st ed. The Anchor Bible, v. 33A. New York: Doubleday.

Miguez, Néstor O. 2010. "Carta a Filemón." In *Comentario Bíblico Latinoamericano—Nuevo Testamento*, edited by Armando

Levarotti, 1043–48. Navarra, Spain: Verbo Divino.

Nicholson, Connie. 2021. "Galatians 3:15-29." Online forum post. Galatians Course, Fresno Pacific Biblical Seminary.

Novenson, V. 2014. "Paul's Former Occupation in Ioudaismos." In *Galatians and Christian Theology: Justification, the Gospel, and Ethics in Paul's Letter,* edited by Mark W. Elliot, Scott J. Hafemann, N. T. Wright, and John Frederick, 24–39. Grand Rapids, MI: Baker Academic.

Richter, Sandra L. 2008. *The Epic of Eden: A Christian Entry into the Old Testament.* Downers Grove, IL: IVP Academic.

Sanders, E. P. 1977. *Paul and Palestinian Judaism: A Comparison of Patterns of Religion.* 1st American ed. Philadelphia: Fortress Press.

Schellenberg, Ryan S. 2003. "New Creation as Canon: Galatians 6:11-18." Unpublished Paper.

———. 2018. "Subsistence, Swapping, and Paul's Rhetoric of Generosity." *Journal of Biblical Literature* 137 (1): 215–34.

———. 2022. Conversation with author about Galatians. Zoom Recording.

Tamez, Elsa. 1993. *The Amnesty of Grace: Justification by Faith from a Latin American Perspective.* Nashville: Abingdon Press.

Witherington, Ben. 1998. *Grace in Galatia: A Commentary on St. Paul's Letter to the Galatians.* Grand Rapids, MI: Eerdmans.

Wright, N. T. 1991. "Putting Paul Together Again: Toward a Synthesis of Pauline Theology." In *Pauline Theology: Vol. 1 Thessalonians, Philippians, Galatians, Philemon,* edited by Jouette Bassler, 183–211. Minneapolis: Fortress Press.

———. 1992. *The Climax of the Covenant: Christ and the Law in Pauline Theology.* 1st Fortress Press ed edition. Minneapolis: Fortress Press.

———. 2004. *Paul for Everyone: Galatians and Thessalonians.* 2nd ed. Louisville, KY: Westminster John Knox Press.

www.ingramcontent.com/pod-product-compliance
Lightning Source LLC
Chambersburg PA
CBHW062048080426
42734CB00012B/2594